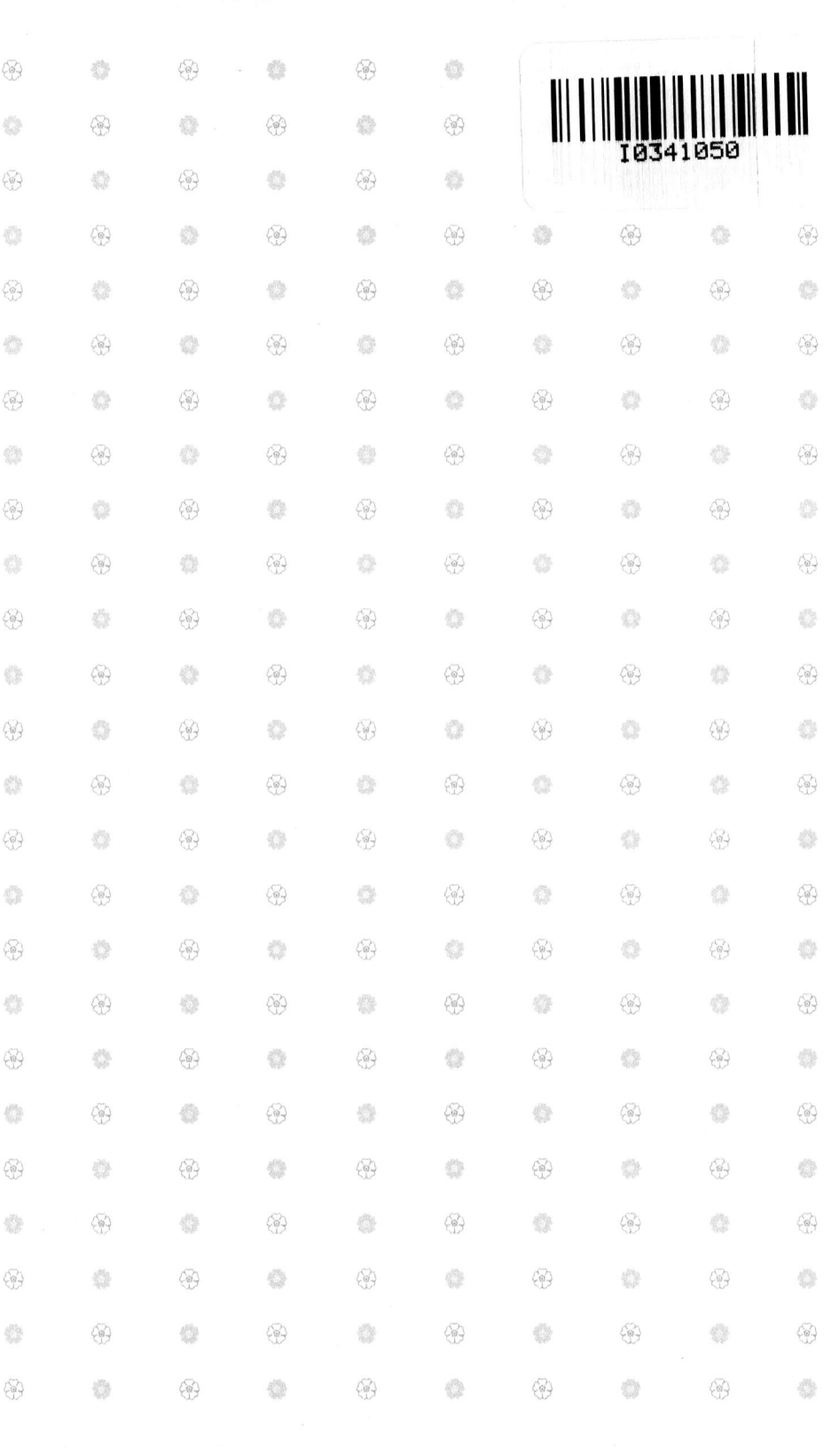

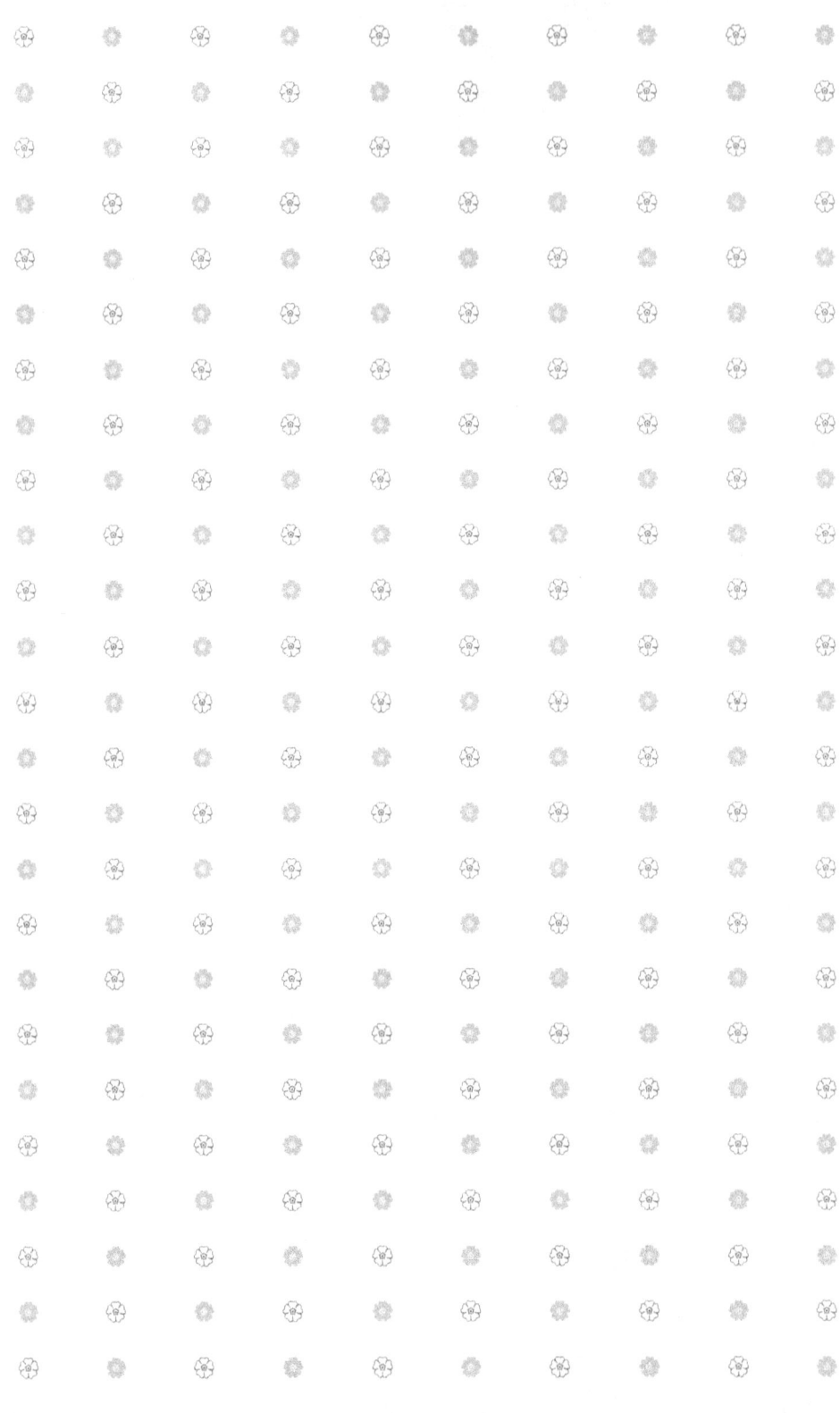

in case of emergency press

We are proud to acknowledge the Traditional Owners of country throughout Australia and to recognise their continuing connection to land, waters, and culture.
We pay our respects to their Elders.

We support recognition, reconciliation, and reparation.

The Sonnets

Howard Firkin

in case of emergency press
https://icoe.com.au
Travancore, Victoria
Australia

Published by in case of emergency press 2023

Copyright © Howard Firkin 2023
All rights reserved. Without limiting the rights under copyright reserved above, no part of this publication may be reproduced, stored in or introduced into a database and retrieval system or transmitted in any form or any means (electronic, mechanical, photocopying, recording or otherwise) without the prior written permission of both the owner of copyright and the publishers.

ISBN: 978-0-6458496-5-3

Table of Contents

Sparrowhawk 1
Fourteen self-explanatory lines 2
No wonder 3
Last train to Dumbsville 4
Cemetery in Lund 5
A mail boy returns to St Kilda Road 6
Love sings 7
Lost Heart 8
Evening Star 9
God saw 10
Male Bonding 11
Prayer of a brick 12
Pocket Australia 13
When a patient is dying 14
Radioinactive 15
Sorted 16
Moving 17
The day that daylight saving ends 18
Universe 19
Tristan's Commission 20
A short note pushed underneath Apollo's door 21
The world returns 22
The easiest addiction 23
The girl with smacked out eyes 24
Postcards from my daughters 25
A letter to Walt (Whitman not Disney) 26
Justice 27
Still in pursuit 28
Somewhere 29
Night sky wanderer 30
Known 31
Aussie Backpackers 32
Richmond Station, Winter 33
The make believe 34
Google air miles 35
How to get on a plane and leave 36
The Only Wisdom 37
Five Hours in Denver 38

Genius 39
Lonely Planeteer 40
Walking in the Botanic Gardens as My Life Was Collapsing Somewhere 41
Backache 42
Button song 43
This dance 44
Watching the tsunami 45
As I lay dying 46
Memories of a blind man 47
Breakdown 48
The children touting 49
Super hero me 50
Another Evening Out 51
The X 52
My wait 53
Copper Man 54
Just walk with me 55
A Modest Proposal for an ex-Mother 56
Shadow Poem 57
Whore writes a sonnet 58
You get depressed 59
A return to poetry 60
Melbourne Cup, 2011 61
Star girl 62
Sick 63
Where's the Denkmal, boys? 64
Lines from songs 65
Still no haemorrhage 66
Tarzan of the Leaf Litter 67
Here 68
Oasis 69
Sort of moon 70
Family Life 71
Drayton's lost sonnet 72
Drawing Lessons 73
Sheffield 74
A long time until morning 75
I've spent my life 76
Hector's letter home 77
An Old Tom Addresses the Great Trade Union of Cats 78
Alphabet Poem 79

Title	Page
Not Written in the Bodleian Library	80
Old Undies	81
Without your silver iteration	82
Accompanists	83
My lover's lover's name	84
Already last week's paper	85
A Thousand Things	86
I Contact	87
Fossil unremarked	88
Winter morning	89
Sonnet 29	90
Longitude	91
Woman with Creutzfeldt-Jakob Syndrome	92
God is my (only) judge	93
Ocean Blue	94
When words run out	95
My life in amber	96
One last poem	97
Death of sorts	98
The Botanic Gardens/ Sparrows/Ruth	99
Eleven minutes later	100
Rain Check	101
Eternal Love, surprisingly	102
First Generation Airbag	103
Here comes the son	104
Whisky ago gone	105
Mars replies to Venus	106
Priest, dying	107
Refugees	108
Teach me to dance	109
Spaceman	110
Love on stage	111
Blue dish cloth	112
Let's all feel sorry for Les	113
Fifth Wheel	114
The only man on Skype	115
Dags and Fat Kids	116
The other judge	117
Then they expect you to pick a career	118
Another nothing	119
Poem in a moleskine journal	120
Paolo's dream of Francesca in the second circle	121

Finishing School	122
Lily	123
The Bequest	124
Summertown, Oxford	125
A Vision of My Dying	126
Firkin's first space walk	127
London	128
Narcissus checks his mobile	129
A snapshot of the day nothing extraordinary happened	130
The Rich and Hungry Still	131
A visit to the Comic's Lounge	132
Australia	133
Vacuum Clean	134
The sculptor's model remembers herself	135
Happy Endings	136
Zoo	137
A Personal Archaeology	138
Leave Me	139
Zombie Diggers, Attack!	140
Bungee walking	141
Hesitation Wounds	142
Phantom Limb	143
The Godless	144
Postcard from Ghent	145
Nicking the Picasso	146
Dog Days	147
Hampstead Heath	148
Postcard to my Dad	149
The deal was truth, absolute truth	150
Returning Virgins	151
She seems now	152
HIV +	153
The river Derci	154
Another of my funerals at Melbourne Uni	155
Universal submission guidelines	156
Perigee moon, Cottesloe Beach, 2011	157
First poem in ten years	158
Ikea Sappho	159
I wave at trains	160
Behind the mirror	161
The Rescue	162
Nothing New (again)	163

Cuneiform	164
Old news at the end of the pier	165
Kristine, because I lost the poems	166
Sex takes sabbatical	167
Four Swallows	168
Time and Motion	169
Lamb	170
It's Pez	171
Cutlery Drawer	172
The differences between me and Shakespeare	173
First Dive	174
The Lost and Con (ten lines of eulogy; four lines of prayer)	175
Prayer at a bus stop	176
The Estate	177
Before the visit to Mad Aunt P.	178
Beograd explained with kajsijevaca	179
Tow Truck	180
The mathematics of your legs	181
Christmas Adam	182
Other men	183
1000W Smile	184
Full stop	185
Discovering the mirror	186
Ukraine 2022	187
Tripwire Town	188
I miss the you	189
Blank white man	190
Her body sprinkles adjectives	191
The Unmapped Hamlet	192
A prayer for George Pell	193
I lived for art	194
Another Way	195
Paralysis	196
Meeting John in Lygon Street	197
Sunset on two trees in different gardens	198
Sugar muse	199
You only use those legs	200
Cat	201
Predictive Text	202
Does anyone know I'm alive?	203
Cathedral of Venus	204
The Serial Farewell	205

The Sugar Generation	206
Woman in burqua	207
Anywhere but here	208
She Never Flips	209
The falconer	210
Because I woke up early	211
When I could fly	212
Perfect black dress	213
The Schwebebahn By Night	214
When you understand	215
And as you age	216
Oxford Physic Garden	217
When other people die	218
25th December at the home	219
Sonnet for a superfluous man	220
Her cat is called Ulysses	221
A first cartographer remembers his lost love in her bath	222
Tranq's for the memory	223
Sunday Morning	224
Sleek	225
Orthodox Christmas Card	226
The secret island	227
Poem for my children	228
Instructions for loneliness	229
Worm	230
In this box	231
Old car	232
Quantum State	233
Well, fuck the fans of Keats	234
You	235
Renaissance Music	236
The Barnacle	237
Woman exercising on Red Rocks beach	238
Butcher Birds	239
I walk your legs	240
Three Thirds of a Day Without You	241
The Apology	244
VA 894	245
The Opening of the New Parliament House by H.R.H. Queen Elizabeth II	246
Sometimes I'm tired	249
A week's awakenings in seven couplets	250

A Hopeless Land	251
Five white shirts	252
Don't Worry, Bob	253
Today	254
Body over time	255
Noosa Beach Retiree	256
Only Scum	257
Painter, retrospective	258
Aphantasia in Geneva	259
Your presence	260
The Doctor's Garden	261
Index of first lines	265

The Sonnets

Howard Firkin

Sparrowhawk

It's complicated. Someone has to talk.
You're waiting... tick, tick, tick... and all my words
are frozen where they perch, like little birds
scared rigid by a circling sparrowhawk.
The moments tick tick tick our lives away.
I lose words in your body. All my lips
can mouth is you, my tongue is tasting, licking,
I hear your voice but feel your warm pulse ticking
and know you've made time fluid and it slips
between the seconds and beyond the day.

It's complicated this. I don't know what
another man would call this. I think bliss
is closest. You are perfect. You think not.
Forget my words. Remember how we kiss.

Fourteen self-explanatory lines

This is the first of fourteen lines that won't
explain the aching beauty of the curve
your bum makes to your thigh or why if I
could choose to be less awkward when I saw
you I'd refuse and take five lines to do it.
I rang you to apologise for being
stupid but apologised for being
instead. You said it sounded like another
line of mine which I denied. I lied.
And so line ten, where nothing is resolved.

Four lines are needed to explain the three
that they contain. The consequence is two
are left alone. If one of them is me,
left here, then that leaves one left there—leaves you.

No wonder

I'm fading: faster than my hair grows grey;
I'm washing left too long out on the line;
I'm last night's salad—look, it still tastes fine;
verandah furniture. I fade away.
It's time that's lending distance to your view.
I'm watching as you rise and grow in light,
as daylight fades and you and other stars
parade around the cafes, clubs, and bars,
and glister photo chemically past night,
becoming brilliant as you always do.

Goodbye's a lengthy process while you wait
for bonds of chemistry to dissipate.
If love is just another change of state,
no wonder grateful one day starts to grate.

Last train to Dumbsville

Of course, the train starts pulling out while we're
still scrambling on, or stuffing racks with cases,
and pushing past each other to our places.
We just can't wait to start our journey there,
apologies and elbows and shy smiles.
Books out or headphones in, or packages
of sandwiches unwrapped, we settle down
and watch the city, field, farmhouse, small town
blur past—steel wheels on steel— it seems it says,
"Dumbsville, Dumbsville, Dumbsville..." for miles and miles.

Against a neighbour's shoulder or the glass,
heads loll, as slowly we succumb to sleep.
It's worth the slight discomfort in your arse,
to know the sweet companionship of sheep.

Cemetery in Lund

You never lived this tidily. Not here;
not even here. You left your beds unmade,
unweeded. Your gravel wasn't always raked.

You left. And some of you, at least, left someone
glad you'd gone. You won't read that in granite,
but some of us read rust and trust its word.

And some of you left families so hurt
they spat your memory on stone to crumble
into lichen coloured flakes. Rake that.

You couldn't and they can't. They leave a flower;
write a poem; drop their tears; and where
the fuck are you? Gone—somewhere past these trees
pollarded into shapes that might mean something,
but don't. A tidy lie. Like you, it's left.

A mail boy returns to St Kilda Road

That's it. The place that launched a thousand miserable careers. I hadn't thought of it in years. The ex-mail boy returning slowly as he dares; a saunter up the pebble-coated stairs to face the great unscene of memory: a boy, a tray, a franking machine, the mail room, mini skirts, and typists who were keen: Joan and Zina, Sue, Janine, where are you all? The reps and clerks gone with the screwed up paper ball of office cricket matches—down which hall? Shane and Pat and Bert and Mister Kimber who retired hurt; his vacant eyes and in-tray seemed to say "In thirty years of service I've done nothing to deserve this…" All gone, but this survives somehow: a building of the nineteen sixties kept its time and place while all around were losing theirs. Who cares? I lost mine with the body shirts, the mining shares, the brown toned suits with wide lapels and hipster flares, patchouli oil, the barbers' chairs, Ted's postal van that had no spare, parmigana, steak tartare, moustaches, sideburns, shag pile hair… our holes so round, our pegs so square. I'm standing in the here and then. You had to be there. Not again.

Love sings

Love sings of love undying even as
it dies. Love knows transition. Love is birth,
the timeless revolutions of the earth.
Love proves the path you take no other has.
Light is and darkness isn't. Love is all.
Four lines define a box. The lines you draw
define the shape, but not the space beyond.
You can't. The infinite does not respond.
The finite is; the infinite is store.
You hear the voice of God each time you call.

Love isn't what you feel—it's why you feel.
Love is the substance. Love defines the true.
There is no ending. What has been is real
and finite as eternity and you.

Lost Heart

Love, it's a lost art. No one knows the craft.
The secrets of the guild are gone for good.
We know there was a time when people could
believe it possible, when no one laughed,
but now? Impossible to contemplate.
We only trust machines to laser cut
computer generated patterns out
to fashion things we've only heard about
in spam from barelylegalasianslut.
You wanted love? Too bad. You've come too late.

We live too long now. Have a look at me:
my DNA's a billion years today.
It still remembers jumping from the tree
and leaving love to walk upright away.

Evening Star

The only star—of course, it's not a star—
with cred is Venus. Why? 'Coz Venus shows.
In dirty city skies, she takes the mike;
reduced to some old rock pub stage she still
gets up and stands before the lights and sings.
She doesn't wonder where her old fans are:
the past is just another song she knows,
a song she sings but doesn't have to like,
'coz someone listening in the darkness will.
She's been around; she's seen her share of things.

As things get easier, as darkness grows,
the other stars and planets deign to dip
their toes in night's declamatory prose,
but Venus sings, alone, and curls her lip.

God saw

And on a later day, God looked again
and saw that it was anything but good:
the forests he'd brought forth no longer stood,
and things he'd made to creep ran like a stain
and covered everything, alive and dead.
"I gave you herbs and fruits for meat. You treat
it all alike—an endless take away!
Did no one ever think they'd have to pay?
Oh, you'll get fries with that, and deep fried meat…"
He started raving. Don't know what he said.

He flipped. Like any burger, any Dad,
who's seen the state the children leave the room.
I wouldn't talk to him right now. He's mad,
but he'll… what starts with 'd' and rhymes with room?

Male Bonding

Conversation in a pub

"I'm not unfaithful to my wife; the girl
friend says I'm polyamorous, that's all...
She says I can't fight nature: it's the call
of semi-wild man's prime need to unfurl
his DNA. You see?" "She has a point,
but not sure that your wife would quite agree..."
"Well, she's content. For her, one man's enough."
"Perhaps, but aren't you worried? Aren't you scared
the new girl might have plans she hasn't shared?"
"What plans?" "You know... like getting up the duff?"
"I've had the snip. Might have to disappoint..."

The drinks go down. "I'll cop you later..." "Bye."
The polyamorist, content with life,
stands, leaves his mate to wonder, "Should I try
to sneak around and slip one to his wife?"

Prayer of a brick

Dear God, let me be missing, crumbled dust,
when others try to recreate this wall.
Let me have been the one which made it fall;
the fissured one that let the damp get just
a sweaty toehold in and kick it down.
You made me mortal, cunt. Well, fine. I'll die.
And you and nothing else will swirl about
not knowing time, and wearing nothing out,
and I won't be and won't have been, won't lie
for you, outline a never had been town.

And you, your brain can trace the molecules
that once were me, and know I was a brick,
and I'll deny it. Liar. Make more fools
and tell them. I'll deny it, God. You prick.

Pocket Australia

for Clive James

Dear Clive, I'm sorry you can't visit; so,
allow me to supply this pocket snap,
a free to download literary app
to keep Australia with you as you go.
Cue magpies, currajongs, and butcher birds.
In smoky green the gum trees nod and wave
like old mates, too long knowing you to rise,
they almost smile, make sure you catch their eyes,
and know you understand the look they gave.
Some feelings never sink as far as words.

Your harbour is as beautiful as sin
conceived in Eden long before a fall.
Sit on its sandstone shores tonight, begin
the farewell that's a greeting to the all.

When a patient is dying

Elisabeth Maranta for the last 18 years has run a Romansh bookshop, Il Palantin, which sells books in Romansh. Asked why most of the books in Romansh she sells are poetry, she muses: "When a patient is dying, he writes only poetry."
New York Times, September 2010.

This is your poem, written in a tongue
that's dying, that will frame its phrases knowing
that no one reads them without stopping, going
to look them up, cornflower blue among
the common yellow maize of commerce words.
To die is to define what can be known.
It never seems a lot because it's not.
That's why the dying cry; it's why death's got
such rotten press: you're bare; your cover's blown:
you know as much as gum trees know of birds.

Somewhere a woman sells another book.
She smiles and wraps it; takes a little cash.
Perhaps this one will read, not simply look.
The fire is remembered in the ash.

Radioinactive

(The speed of life)

The crickets trill like geiger counters, stopping
as I pass. I'm radioinactive,
emitting nothing, inert, unattractive;
my half-life started low and just keeps dropping,
decaying many times the speed of life.
The nucleus of being is the ache,
the poisoned tooth that shoots electric bolts
of pain across your skull—ten thousand volts
for each and every infantile mistake.
If God's wrath 's not a sword, it's one big knife.

A cricket starts to tick, resets the beat;
the same atomic pulse since life began.
It echoes in your footsteps down the street.
You think you'll walk away. You never can.

Sorted

This is a very human trait: we sort,
we classify, we name, divide and join,
define and re-define in terms we coin
to never quite explain the things we thought
could only be explained with words (which don't).
The other very human trait: we sort
of make it up when nothing works the way
it should, when all the words we have convey
no more than that we know less than we ought.
We'll try to get it right next time. We won't.

I want to tell you, but I'd have to use
these words, or some words similar, and they
unclarify, they re-obscure, confuse;
so while I sort my thoughts, think words I say.

Moving

(The new house)

I'm staying here—immovable as debt.
I'm never leaving, never going to try.
I stay. And when the floor sags, so will I:
I will grow comfortable; I will forget
the dreams I never had the will to prove.
And I will sit all summers in the garden
and drink cold beer and listen to the stars
sing like mosquitoes. Comet tails of cars
will trace the freeway. Arteries will harden.
And I will age and die and never move.

Intention is a fickle kite to fly—
I know the best laid slabs can shift and crack—
but while the reel still holds the odd coil I
look forward to a flight of looking back.

The day that daylight saving ends

The day that daylight saving ends and I'm
the only person in the city late—
last fish to spawn; the river at its spate—
it's me against the clock, man versus time.
I think we can predict a nil-one score.
Perception slows with age, so time speeds up.
My heart beats faster; breath grows shorter;
the ground beneath my feet has turned to water;
I spill food down my front, upset my cup.
Clocks can't be bothered lying any more.

From somewhere in reflections, old age winks,
and smiles, its gums withdrawn around its teeth,
obscene and certain—no one thinks
that time will beggar all: love and belief

Universe

The everlasting universe of things,
the physical, the real, the things we touch,
the things we gather, throw, or trust to clutch,
the treasure and the rubbish Santa brings,
these things dissolve the other worlds we dream.
The petals of those worlds fall down, arc right
and left and fall, a tiny, fragile storm:
disperse, collect, shift, settle, move, reform,
and shatter into something—stars at night,
or flecks of mica making granite gleam.

You know I never think of you by choice.
Last night I dreamt of you—your skin, your eyes—
and let the birdsong logic of your voice
transfuse me with the plasma of old lies.

Tristan's Commission

Couldn't be easier. As easy as
a hand upon my shoulder. It's a lark.
The trusted one. The loyal me. The mark
of royal favour which no other has.
You ask me what could possibly go wrong?
I'll tell you. Nothing. That great nothing which
is blankly squatting, basalt in my heart,
the vacuum of the sealed room, the part
unfinished tapestry, the golden stitch,
which shines in coming and which can't be long.

Look, I'm no seer, but even I can tell
this potion thing is not a good idea:
her eyes, her hands, her smile, a woman's smell
are potion. Right, let's go. The skies are clear.

A short note pushed underneath Apollo's door

My dear, ambiguous God/poet/ess,
I miss you, and I miss the words I'd find
you'd hidden in the hidden folds of mind.
I miss the way you loved me, more or less.
Your lesson learned: less lessens to its end.
I'm left without you, left without the sun
you give to someone else. I'm left without
the words to tell what's left to talk about,
and who'd be here to hear it told? No one.
You don't reply. A God is not a friend.

Your voice I still hear, all the old, sad songs
that once amused me. Now the words apply.
Immortals cannot love—no man belongs
with you—but I will love you as I die.

The world returns

(putting on my specs)

It's there again. The world. It's back. The leaves
are individual and not a smear,
reflections on the window re-appear,
the furniture resolves, the brain perceives.
And you've gone nowhere, centred in the real
and always centre of imagination,
the always only thought, forever there.
The world returns and frames you: face and hair.
The world is curling ribbon—presentation.
The only permanent is what I feel.

The world is back projection; you're the star.
It's always you who's filling centre screen.
My poor sight helps me see you as you are:
the real, the woman otherwise unseen.

The easiest addiction

I see you and the scales form on my eyes:
the milky soft, the vaseline glass view;
the definition of perfection: you.
It leaves no way to see you otherwise.
The easiest addiction is a lie.
Your words ignite the molecules of blood
which dance around my body, flush my brain
with song, erasing memories of pain.
I float on, drown in your endorphin flood.
Don't want to breathe; don't even want to try.

The morning hangover: I didn't die;
my self still in the flesh it occupies.
Your words are words again, left as they lie.
I see you and the scales form on my eyes.

The girl with smacked out eyes

Experience has taught you how to look
the other way: inwards. Your world is whole,
of universes, it's one you control.
Your mind is its own author, reader, book—
all else is nothing, distant as the stars.
Not begging, selling, not in any way
involved, your life's evolved beyond the touch
of friends, of lovers, anybody much...
Who touches you? You really couldn't say.
Not men you suck off, hunched in family cars.

You walk past. Bird through cloud. Oblivious
and beautiful. You walk and disappear
and leave the obvious, lascivious,
the tedious. You leave. We stay. Left here.

Postcards from my daughters

My children send me postcards from a land
where horizontal threes hang in the sky
beneath a golden hedgehog. It can fly
like anything—the ground's there if you stand,
but gravity's no law, and okay rules.
The houses there sport jaunty chimneys, smoke
is worn in perfect ringlets, gardens grow
their flowers in a single level row,
and everybody's smiling at the one joke:
at me and all outlandish bloody fools.

Relentlessly they travel on and stop
for nothing less than night—their only care
is not to miss their journey's end. They drop
the odd line home, and wish I could be there.

A letter to Walt (Whitman not Disney)

I saw the best lines of my generation
contort, then wither, wrinkle, scorch, and burn:
I saw their thin flames flare, subside, and turn
to ash. The furnace of your declamation
too fierce, too constant, too damn bloody hot.
So Walt, I'm leaving off my reading now.
Back to your shelf. Back to the dog-eared school
anthologies. Impress the kids—they're cool
with old poofs now, or say so, anyhow,
but pricks like me resent the hold you've got.

The young will worship still—same every age—
our one defence: to smile and criticise,
and glower, feverless in lukewarm rage,
and covet, curse, and claim, and plagiarise.

Justice

Just ice without the alcohol, just speed
without the high... It's what you might call pretty
pointless—thoughts of you and feeling shitty...
Forever unresolved: desire and need.
    I realise this doesn't make much sense.
But memories are losing definition,
the symptoms now are milder than before,
the pocks are less volcanic though still sore,
and each infection marks a new remission:
    attacks of you become their own defence.

I can't afford the feelings I once had—
you're not worth one last night out on the piss.
Like all the worst songs of Anon & Trad,
you don't deserve forgetting, lover. Just this.

Still in pursuit

I'm chasing you, if only slowly; I'm
still in pursuit and every step you take,
each baulk and side-step, every shift and fake,
delays your capture, not your fate. The time
is coming, little one. The dance must end.
I see the footsteps painted on the floor.
I hear the music, feel you sway your hips.
I notice everything: the little slips,
the way you dance—no longer quite as sure.
Be certain, darling girl, I'm not your friend.

We know whose arm you feel around your waist;
the music slows; you know it's growing late.
Your steps pretend to flight, but you are chased
and you will fall. You know it. I can wait.

Somewhere

... so somewhere in the world it's half past twelve,
a number almost nothing rhymes with—good
work there—so surely both of us (read: you) could
find it in your protocol to shelve
(phew!) those flint-hearted plans of yours to work
and call me, think of me, and write a line
to make my head spin, words that make my skin
react as if to breath, to sunlight, pin,
some quiet words that put the shhhh in shine,
that change the irk of work, that let me shirk.

Okay, I'm feeling silly. Like a kid.
I wouldn't let another see this. This
is yours, the silliness, the light—you did
this to me. Thanks. My line to you this: x

Night sky wanderer

The woman tracing her erratic way
along the footpaths, through suburban night,
her footsteps leaving green night-vision light
of warmth and love, leaves traces of a day
she lit with presence, working, laughter, all.
The footpaths stamped with leaves, her envelopes
containing secret, folded thoughts, the steps
away, toward, around. Each path accepts
its walker tapping out her dreams, her hopes,
as skies allow their stars to shine or fall.

She has a destination, not a route;
a vision, not a map; she's journeying.
Her thoughts are honed, obtuse becomes acute,
alive becomes her living and her being.

Known

We both know you're not reading this and I'm
not writing now. Another reads. Hello,
unknown. So how am I supposed to know
what words to write to you and you-in-time
and other you? We both know nothing's known.
When you were very small, when you first learnt
that things had names that you could mispronounce,
and swallowed their prevention's bitter ounce
of pounding cure and had your fingers burnt,
when you were very small, what were you shown?

I saw a curtain move and almost part.
I saw a flame. I saw wax turned to grime.
We both knew our same nothings from the start,
but now I understand it: nothing's time.

Aussie Backpackers

You've got to love Australian girls abroad.
They're cool. They're up for it. They're obvious.
They're raucous: "Hey! Tonight! Come up and see us!";
or let themselves be asked, cajoled, implored.
They share their lives the way they'd share a meal.
They treat me like an uncle—borrow cash
and tell me who's got lucky and with whom,
their paparazzi eyes dance round the room
and everything is photographed with flash—
a little crisper, brighter than is real.

If Europe is a cold, dark pool, they know
they're water candles on it. When they're gone
they're leaving less than ripples here to show
how they ignited life with love and shone.

Richmond Station, Winter

Melancholy: stations do a good
line in it. People huddle, drag on smokes,
or wring cold hands. Announcements like bad jokes
that no one gets. Lost platform souls who could
be somewhere else—but always, there's a catch.
Remembering because there's time to spend:
this is a boyhood scene, the jigsaw fits
a piece, the Rorschach blot of missing bits
is one bit smaller, closer to that end
when box and puzzle finally don't match.

The trains arrive, the sets of people change.
Pursuing private ends which they suppose
to be of purpose, faces/bodies rearrange
and something—not timetabled, not known—flows.

The make believe

It's just a game: we hide; we seek; we find;
we don't reveal. And while we play, it's real,
and that's the point—we make believe we feel
until we do and brain submits to mind.
It's your turn. Close your eyes and count to ten.
You hear me move. Did I say something? What?
Your counting is a metronome, heart beat,
slow drumming of your fingers, tapping feet,
a dripping tap. You're coming, ready or not,
and I am hiding, waiting, found again.

Our nakedness our only hiding place,
the only place we never have to leave.
We disappear from others without trace,
but that's the magic, that's the make believe.

Google air miles

You're never more than Google million miles
away and so you ought to feel all right,
she says, or would say were she here tonight.
She's not. She's under someone else's smile;
her belly's under someone else's hands.
I should be earning points or air miles, surely.
I'm paying, getting nothing in return
for all the aviation fuel I burn:
her loyalty programme rewards me poorly—
an outcome every traveller understands.

If distance lends estrangement to us two,
we're many thousand lifetimes' space apart.
And yet you're imminent. I'm close to you
with each click of my taxi meter heart.

How to get on a plane and leave

Pack everything you want to leave behind
in boxes, bags, in piles beneath the bed,
in letters, texts, in things you've left unsaid,
and once packed up, dismiss them from your mind.
Now, grab an empty bag, some cash, and go.
I see your body sketched in sweeps of form,
in softened, charcoaled lines that fool my seeing
to hope for touch, and scent, to look for being,
to feel your skin, sweat-smooth, hair-soft, bed-warm;
that hope is past hope. You are gone, I know.

You were, to me, as beautiful as light:
you weren't the flower, but the way it shone.
Your face, your voice, your walk return each night,
but you, forever only one, you're gone.

The Only Wisdom

This journey starts without a leaving and
will end without arriving; you will sail
the blue-black sea in search of land and fail.
The sea is shoreless and there is no land.
Acceptance is the only wisdom here.
Although the ocean is infinity,
the stars—the visible, at least—are not,
and they confirm you sail the course you plot.
Of course, direction is a fallacy:
a point is any point; that much is clear.

The charts we use are fanciful and false.
They promise us horizons we won't see
but seek, impelled to trust the aching pulse
that guides us to our pointless finity.

Five Hours in Denver

For Charlotte

The dry stone wall is built of many rocks,
none uniform and none the same, their shape
dictates position in the final wallscape,
but not utility—each is a block
that shapes the choice and function of the next.
This wasted time in Denver is one stone,
one pebble in a wall that reaches back
beyond first memories to somewhere black,
beyond forgetting and beyond the known,
but beautiful as hieroglyphic text.

My little one, whatever your life builds—
a wall, a garden, house, a book, a song—
don't doubt your life makes you uniquely skilled
to build it. Never doubt. Be always strong.

Genius

So go. But understand you'll never know
another mediocre genius.
The semi-spirit which transfigured us
is gone, flame-fled, dead match head, candle, blow,
you know the story: Once upon the end.
Now you can mix with better, sparkling spirits.
We mediocre can be left to croon
our three chord melodies and moon spoon June
our vinyl feelings. You don't need to hear it.
But thank you from a once transfigured friend.

You made me shine, bees wax on antique wood,
like something luminous. You made me glow.
The sheen has gone, but, sweetheart, it was good
to be your shining light-like something. Go.

Lonely Planeteer

So now the rain decides to tumble down,
uncritical applause to end a day
that no one should have noticed anyway—
another hotel room, another town,
another language I will never speak.
We children of the book live by one law:
no days shall be allowed to be alike.
"Enjoy a quirky local tour by bike…"
"Explore the vibrant hawkers' stalls before…"
I still observe, but faith is growing weak.

No guidebook recommends you turning back.
It never says on page one: "Stay in bed."
I can't be bothered even to unpack.
This town's too much like something that I read.

Walking in the Botanic Gardens as My Life Was Collapsing Somewhere

It's just another blackbird in the leaves
that's making sudden footsteps off the path,
another ring-eyed lunatic who needs
a few deep breaths before he falls apart
and falls again upon those softer lives.
A family meets family. They move
around and through and reassemble past—
the trees hang leaves into the lake and smooth
their own reflections from it—for their part
the children swap quick glances, husbands wives.

Another turn before it's night or spring...
like all of us they're just around the bend...
Tomorrow's birds will feed here, preen, and sing,
and love affairs surprise us all and end.

Backache

All right, you bastard bloody thing, you've beaten me.
You win. I'm pinned and prostrate. Will you please get off
and give the drugs some dulling time to do their work?
Come on. Allow me leave, at least, to look at you.
Relax your claws, unclasp, unhook and clamber round
where I can see you. Surly thing. Unsightly, ugly
thing. There. Now I know you: many knobble-jointed,
many limbed and lined and loose-linked thing.
I'd like to slide a skewer through that shiny skin
and pierce you, crack your carapace, or crush you flat
to watch you ooze life through your shell and lose your grip,
your hold on me. It might inspire momentary
pity, but I bet it wouldn't. Bastard thing.
You win. So scuttle softly back and sink your teeth.

Button song

Cross little faces singing their complaint:
they know your fingers but they're kept away
from other skin. They hide that skin for you
and you accept their service but don't offer
their reward: your body. You just flirt
with them, caress their smooth round bodies, poke
them through the button holes and then forget
them, peel your blouse off, drop it to the floor
and welcome someone else to kiss your breasts.
Discarded faces, knowing they will have
to serve again when you pick up your shirt
and toss it round your shoulders, push your arms
through sleeves and use your fingers, torture them,
insert them, tug, and make them bear that strain.

This dance

This dance—this tapping on the keys, these hands
exploring you, exploring thought, defining
words defining you, the words refining
your description: adjectives and ands,
the nouns, the punctuation—this dance kills me.
Each tiny insect heart pulse, micro beat,
amoebic movements, lashing flagellates,
these dot and dash flash scraps of meaning, cognates
of the universal, incomplete
descriptor dance notation—this dance fills me.

Where are you dancing now? Today? This minute?
Who else holds you in body or in thought?
I thought I watched the dance and wasn't in it,
but everybody's watching, dancing, caught.

Watching the tsunami

Impossibly innocuous, it comes
as black as lava, sulphurous with dreams
and debris, boiling, oily rubble teems
across the landscape screens and numbs.
This can't be, as it stares us in the face.
Immediate and future, nothing stops
and everything is gone, as blank as silt,
the tumbled coloured blocks a child has spilt,
the tiny chaos when a tea tray drops,
destruction of the sacred commonplace.

We see the images. They don't make sense.
We hear the words: they surge and wash around,
incomprehensible; our last defence:
abandonment of light and touch and sound.

As I lay dying

As I lay dying, I remembered you.
I wanted you to know, but also knew,
it didn't matter, news would filter through,
or not, but time takes care of what is true,
and dying, truth is obvious and all.
I felt you with me. You were there and I
could hold your hand, could touch that silky skin
again, and all I never thought to try
was tried, remembered, loved, and held within
a shared, a conjured gospel of recall.

As I lay dying, I abandoned pain
and hope. Within my chest the air
diffused, sunlight transfused me, through my veins.
I didn't float. I was. And you were there.

Memories of a blind man

I don't remember faces well, it's true.
And voice is treacherous: it comes and goes.
And smell needs trigger smells—don't trust your nose,
but let my hands run gently over you
and I'll identify you—guaranteed.
Let's see, the neck is smooth, the shoulders square,
the breasts are soft, the nipples rising, formed
to perfect peaks, the belly soft and warmed
as if by rising heat, let me check there...
and now I know you: you're the one I need.

I kiss your flesh, your perfume dances through
my head. I kiss your lips and feel your tongue
caress my lips and memories of you
wring words and music, heard, remembered, sung.

Breakdown

(Dead fish on a dirty shore)

I'm washed up, dead, sea-spat upon this shore,
flesh marked with evolution's pinking shears,
the jaws and teeth of forty million years
that shaped themselves to shape and shred before
they lost their meal to sand and air and tide.
I'm melting into sand. Recombinant,
I fray into the stinking soup of air,
a fug that impregnates your clothes, your hair,
the semen taste of death's adulterant.
Organic chemistry won't be denied.

The small mouths will return to me at night,
unweaving threads and picking cartilage clean.
Before you leave, inhale the smell and sight:
ingest me. I was something that had been.

The children touting

(What's on fire?)

The street is full; unnoticed miracles
are hustling. Footpaths are a stage; stars shine
in cameos against the brickwork. Night
comes floating down like feathers when a bird
is shot in flight, or perfume from a doorway.
The children peek out of their hiding places:
the adult bodies they cohabit, faces
illegible as hope—the counterfeit
they deal in. "Mister?" all they need to ask
you with the moistened question mark you hear
a dozen times in thirty silver yards.

Walk past the jaundiced moon left burning there,
the dollar coin you spot beneath the bench
but can't decide to pick up. What's on fire
to fill the air with this peculiar stench?

Super hero me

Don't think, because I never wear a cape,
I don't have super powers. I have one:
the power to leave important things undone—
on life's keyboard, not Enter but Escape.
When you need things ignored, babe, I'm your man.
Look there! Up in the sky! Is it a bird?
Yes, it's a bird. I'm sitting on my arse
while buildings burn, and kids are shot in class,
volcanoes blowing, villages interred—
I'm doing nothing. Why? Because I can.

I never made the dash out of the phone booth;
if I saved anybody, no one saw.
Keep looking, kid—I'm telling God's own truth—
if inspiration's what you're looking for.

Another Evening Out

Her clothes are one of her obsessions. I'm
not. Lovers take up wardrobe space and time
she hasn't got to spare—she's twenty-eight—
you may not like it but you'll wear it, mate.
    She stands before the mirror, pats her hips.
We're just another couple here and speak
above the other couples of the week
we've spend apart: she tells me what she wants,
and nothing changes but the restaurants.
    Her words are an excuse to watch her lips.

She drops me home. She's halfway down the street
before the bad gear change that's her goodbye.
At home she'll let the dress fall round her feet—
she's leaving all obsessions where they lie.

The X

The X waits like a spider in the dark
recesses of an alphabet she wants
to head: a signature of ignorance,
a blight, infecting any spot she marks,
a symbol of my every damn mistake.
She knits her filthy skeins because she must
convince herself and friends she's trapping game.
If only she could work out who's to blame:
her most elaborate webs collect most dust,
and no one gives her what she says she'll take.

Suspended venom in a bulb of flesh—
her toxins all that she can call her own—
she waits for someone to embrace her mesh
of sticky lies, and prove she's not alone.

My wait

Regrets? I've had a feud with my past life.
We hate each other; each one wants to kill
the other—but we don't and never will—
the ties that bind too strong for any knife,
and so we hobble on, me and my past.
Because I drag around so much of what
has gone before, I'm clumsy and I move
like something viscous, like I disapprove
of youth's fluidity, of what they've got
that if I ever had, could not make last.

I'm growing slowly but enormously.
My flesh is pooling, fat lies wave on wave
around my belly, heart, each artery;
caught in its undertow, I can't be saved.

Copper Man

What's that? What's hiding in your kitchen clutter?
What's buried in that drawer of carving forks
and ladles, tongs and chopsticks, plastic corks?
A little copper man, a biscuit cutter:
as golden as the morning sun in Perth.
In early languages, the lost ones, gold
and copper shared a single word with sun.
These either ores were sun on earth, the one
was hard, the other soft; both metals told
and proved the sun once walked upon the earth.

We open every drawer we ever shut.
I feel your palm along my body's length:
you press me into dough; my shape is cut
into your skin: our sun; our single strength.

Just walk with me

Just walk with me where rock shelves poke red tongues
out to the sea and shelter lives as countless
as the stars, significant as ours.

Just walk with me through crowds of eucalypts,
their litter at our feet, their noisy rush
of leaves, big city in their scorn of us.

Just walk with me through air that sounds like gravel,
electric and alive and booming like
artillery and sweet with coming rain.

Just walk with me, insist on your opinion,
press your hand upon my forearm, talk
as if you chose your words, as if they meant.

Just walk with me and scuff time's foreshore for us,
indelible, and pay no mind to tide.

A Modest Proposal for an ex-Mother

This might work: tear them, like you tear a sheet
of paper, into pieces, so they'll fit
into your handbag. When you go to meet
your hireling Solomon each handy bit
is coin in which rage can be quantified.
"A piece half that was recently accorded
enough for any father; I advise
ask more: the heart routinely is awarded
to mum; no, leave the spleen; yes, take the eyes."
Where none looks to forgive, our laws divide.

Your children will remain forever little;
you'll wizen, grey with lying, and depart,
a mist about your mouth, a spray of spittle;
the damp fog of a nugatory heart.

Shadow Poem

These are not words. These are the shadows cast
when one meets zero. Binary. The light/
its absence. Binary. You cannot write
without a (power) point. Words must have passed
into the future when we weren't aware.
Words used to live in skin. Words used to smell
of printers ink, their pages stained with tea
or curried fingerprints. They used to be;
they were—there when the book was closed as well—
and now they're not. They're nothing: absenceware.

This only is a poem while you choose.
It lives like perfume on another's skin.
This poem leaves you nothing left to lose:
it ends whenever you decide: begin.

Whore writes a sonnet

I need a sign: THIS ISN'T LOVE, okay?
Love's just another item on the list:
no anal, bondage, drugs, no being kissed,
no love. You pay, you come, I leave, you stay.
And neither of us gets to change the rules.
I'm not your friend. I'm doing this for me.
And no, you cannot ask me why. I'd lie
before I told you anyway. Don't try.
And don't think anything is yours for free.
I don't do conversation—not with fools.

I'm here because you asked me, not because
I want to be with you. You're anyone.
There's no one else but you. I wish there was
but that's an old dream. Stop. Let's get this done.

You get depressed

Yes, I'm talking to you.

You get depressed because you're stunning? What?
You get depressed because the world won't wake
to give you things that you've refused to take?
What's there to give that you can't say you've got?
Look in the mirror. Tell me, what's your beef?
You are as beautiful as rainy days,
black pepper on a poached egg; you're the taste
of hollandaise and caper berries placed
on folds of salmon, gleaming champagne glaze.
Your only lack: the germ of self-belief.

They'll whisper, make tut-tutting noises, cough.
So what? It's still you standing centre stage,
and all the business, staging, noises off,
will win you your applause (and feed their rage).

A return to poetry

All right. I wasn't always faithful; nor
were you. It's true. When I went looking for
the answers no one's found, you didn't teach
me anything I couldn't learn from each
of other sad addictions: so I left.
I left and told the story to the less
than caring few who asked or tried to guess.
I lived the ex-life, heard of you through friends,
and bent my loneliness to suit my ends:
an agile cripple, blind and dumb and deft.

You'll say that this remains a young man's game.
You're right, of course, and yet I celebrate
that lovers are alike, but not the same,
and every love that starts defies its fate.

Melbourne Cup, 2011

A helicopter chops a potentate
across the skies. Below, on Racecourse Road,
the guys assist their girlfriends to unload
the champagne chicken breakfasts that they ate.
The ladies totter on, discarding heels.
Tomorrow is a work day, but tonight
can fill with memories of silky flanks,
of whispered promises and urgent thanks,
of dreams that everything will be all right
with only mildly compromised ideals.

Tomorrow's paper will remind us which
horse won, re-run the whole race stride by stride,
reminding all how nearly they were rich,
but nothing really happened. No one died.

Star girl

for Jenny, leaving

Hey star girl! Where you heading now? And where
do you imagine needs your sparkle more
than here? I've asked them: everybody's sure
where you belong—and no one wants to share
with others more than we already do!
Hey star girl. Sweet, intense, and lovely one.
Don't go. Get better. Don't leave now. Not yet.
Those future star girl fans you haven't met,
and those you have—so much remains undone
and all of us, we want it done with you.

Goodbye, sweet-hearted girl. You must be gone.
I should want you to free yourself. I don't.
But go. Just one less star to wish upon.
The universe may darken, but you won't.

Sick

Heart sick, brain sick, soul sick. I cannot live
like this. I'm cell sick to my inmost core—
can't stomach my reflection anymore,
can't stand the sight, sound, smell of me. Forgive
me nothing. Nothing's all you'll get.
My stomach bubbles nausea, a pot
of bones, fat, greasy stock on rolling boil,
its smell coats everything in rancid oil.
I vomit nothing. Nothing's all I've got.
Do you recall those things which I forget?

While everybody smiles and makes polite
demands and ask why they don't see me more,
I'm trapped in slow and ever darker night
to twist and retch bile slime up on the floor.

Where's the Denkmal, boys?

(written after a visit to the Denkmal für die ermordeten Juden Europas, Berlin 2010)

In Berlin they can stomach them. So where's
the Denkmal for the boongs? Don't they deserve
it yet? A somewhere we can go observe
a moment's peace? Somewhere the nation shares
its grief for all our unrecorded crimes?
It's not enough to mumble sorries. One
day we must mark in stone, in time, in light,
our knowledge: we can never make this right,
but we can tell the future what was done,
accepting judgement of those future times.

Our history is not our map. It's just
the road remembered, but if we forget,
if we can't recognise faint tracks in dust,
then we deserve the future that we'll get.

Lines from songs

They sting: the lines you sing when things are dark;
the words that someone wrote for money and
a girl; the lines that didn't work back then
and don't work now, but still hit home, hit hard.
I don't work either. Everything's a line.
You tell me... what? You tell me words and I
respond with... what? With words... and having strung
my bead words, don't they sound like something sung,
like something very like another lie?
I wouldn't know. It's all... what? All... what? Fine.

It stings. It hurts. It makes me want to cry.
It makes me want to hold you, smell your hair.
It makes me want to tell you... what? That I
don't make a lot of sense without you there.

Still no haemorrhage

Dear Granddad Mullens, whom I never knew,
today, a headache—still no haemorrhage.
I guess that's good. I'm closing on your age
and fate—the one I'm looking forward to:
I proffer thanks, Saint Paracetamol.
Dear Grandad Mullens, whom I never met,
would you have had advice for me? Were you
the one I needed to have listened to,
those words that I was never to forget?
Well, that explains a lot if not the whole.

Dear Grandad Mullens, though we never spoke,
tonight, some night, at least, come back, explain
before the punch line of your gene line's joke,
before my heart bleeds night into my brain.

Tarzan of the Leaf Litter

The only life I've left is locked in your
imagination, where it seems I'm free
to live the wild life, swing from tree to tree
and beat my chest and live by jungle law.
It's grand… it's cinematic… just not real.
I scurry into undergrowth. I'm lost
in shadow, in the leaf litter, alert
for crawling things, mouth full of worms and dirt:
a feast for your Lord of the Jungle Compost.
Imagine a Colossus. Make him kneel.

I'm always tired. Every rustle, crack,
each flicker of a leaf, a breeze, all make me start.
I'm tensed and scared, expecting the attack:
the final thrust, the spear impales the heart.

Here

    Here is where the homeless heart is stuck
in peak hour traffic. Here two million lives
are choking as they fume. A million wives,
a million husbands couldn't give a fuck.
Their one thought ticking over in the thick air:
    Get me there! Away… where fingers worm
about the thick soil in and under roots
to plant imaginary seasons' fruits
(those bumper crops), where annual's a term
of hope, where being is the only prayer.

I can't say where you'll find me winding up.
All roads lead anywhere you choose to steer.
I've had it with this life. I'm winding up
the windows and I'm getting out of here.

Oasis

Don't make the desert's worst mistake, mistake
this beautiful oasis being just
another dry mirage: more ash and dust.
This may be unexplained; it isn't fake.
The heat distorts our sight, but love restores;
so trust you heart on days you can't trust eyes—
your 3D vision never was too hot—
so trust the 1D vision we've both got:
accept each miracle without surprise,
accept the cool, the water, palms, the pause.

And sit with me as we restore our sight
with desert skies that darken into dream,
removed from journeying for just one night,
our stars—oasis points of light—our stars gleam.

Sort of moon

It orbits and it shines a silver light
on everything; a sort of moon; a sort
of greyscale presentation giving thought
a physical reality that might
mean we can tread the streets that either dreams.
I see you walking, stopping past the trees
to harvest light to check your watch. You stand
and look around. I'm here. I wave a hand.
I call, but I'm the watcher no one sees
and you're an image. Nothing's as it seems.

At least in monochrome I see you here.
I watch the way your bum waves its goodbye.
Your heels tap their remorse code loud and clear,
and leave me here to want to sort of die.

Family Life

The parents watch the tele while the kids
stare at their phones. This is the life we share.
We're close enough to breathe each other's air,
but separately distant. Distance rids
enchantment from our viewing, leaves us mute.
Where once we looked for images in fire,
or traced the spiral of a falling leaf
to clarify our smoke wisps of belief,
to coddle, soothe, assuage, delight, inspire,
belief is lost to facts we can't refute.

We're living in Pompeii. Vesuvius
is pumping filth and fury through the sky.
We stare at glass, preserved, oblivious—
don't even think to wish our loves goodbye.

Drayton's lost sonnet

You're not alone when you are still alone.
I am. No other drums impatiently,
mitosing in my body cavity.
I'm left here, singularly on my own,
in contrast to the very plural you.
I listen to the sounds that never cease—
self-replicating strings are never still.
The cleaving blankness grows like second will,
preparing for our mutual release,
which it will trigger when it's ready to.

Meanwhile, you'll decorate in pastels, comb
through catalogues and play the faithful wife
who picks a name and brings the picked name home.
Leave me alone. Go make your other life.

Drawing Lessons

(the vanishing point)

The unseen lines draw you, and you are made,
drawn somewhere outside inside, to a point
where disparate is unacknowledged, joint,
where light is one variety of shade,
but you are there, unvanished; you persist.
The here is undefined, unfound, removed,
the rumoured world, imagined by a drunk,
the shrunken head kept in a sailor's trunk,
repulsive, possible but never proved,
a nightmare no one says cannot exist.

The paper doesn't predicate the frame,
the gilt, the glass, the wire, the picture hook.
A smudge can make a drawing worth the name.
You only vanish every time I look.

Sheffield

The Sheffield soot is being washed away.
It's disappearing from the brick and stone
and leaving new apartments you can own,
appliance stores, street stalls on market day,
night clubs, and tourist buses. Is this strange?
I wanted steel grey skies. I wanted blades.
I wanted grime and something that explained
an absence. Nothing did. At least it rained.
At least, I think it did. The picture fades
as memories and futures interchange.

The only thing that I can say about
the town I thought I'd see: it wasn't there.
Developers have cleared the foundries out,
and absence breathes its poison through the air.

A long time until morning

It's been a long time since I felt like this,
a long time. Is it you or me? I can't
select a pronoun or convincing reason.
Can you? Can you explain? Can you at least
confirm that something happened? If so, what?
And how did that—whatever—change each day
so each day's different now? Where is it hidden?
This something, who's it hidden from? Not you.
You. You have everything. You're beautiful.
You're luminous, as beautiful as cloud,
as perfume, a piano chord, a flame.
You're beautiful as reason: breathe on me.
Resuscitate me. Kiss me. Let me kiss you.
Let me see you—beautiful as morning.

I've spent my life

I've spent my life. Not well or wisely. Not
with any sense of having really spent it.
I think I sort of hoped I'd only lent it,
but what is left me turns out all I've got,
and all turns rapidly to nothing more.
I can't be trusted with the simplest task.
I never learnt my tables, never will.
I don't remember birthdays. Always spill
your darkest secrets—no one has to ask.
Can't bat; can't bowl; can't throw; and can't keep score.

When I review my life, there's nothing there.
Time used me to confirm that it could pass.
I was a brief disturbance of the air,
a greasy smear left on the mirror glass.

Hector's letter home

Adored wife and the armour that I wear,
forgive the brevity of this. You know
my words, you know how all the old songs go:
their words are mine. Sing them and I am there.
Kiss both our sons: the born; the yet to be.
Adored wife, as I write, I feel you here.
When I am tired (as I am tonight),
my memories of you are new, are foresight,
a dream, as fresh as water and as clear.
I sleep with you tonight, as you with me.

One day we'll work out how to measure time
that isn't meaningless: the time I spend
with you in bed, in thought, in dreams, in rhyme.
Until that time, unmeasured, time can't end.

An Old Tom Addresses the Great Trade Union of Cats

Comrades! The call to strike is a mistake!
All right, we're all aware the vote will go
against me ... Stop yammering and let me take
a moment of your time to tell you so.
    These moonlit autumn nights are dangerous.
Nobody doubts your motives. We all feel
the cold, rough tongue of winter through our coats.
You cry for change and I applaud your zeal,
but seasons change without regard for votes,
    and winter will remain a plague on us.

There was a time I could have held the floor.
I fought and fornicated... now I sleep.
I'm finished. Have your vote. You'll learn for sure:
cat food is still expensive, mouse traps cheap.

Alphabet Poem

It's very like the periodic table:
the alphabet contains the universe,
and pluriverse, and all the other verse.
It's all there: every line that you were able
to write, remember, recollect, regret.
The elements of style, of savoir faire,
of awkward syllables of guilt, of pain,
the a to z of trying to explain,
the how and why it turned out you weren't there;
the alphabet ensures you can't forget.

Arrange yourselves. Like leaves. Like dice. Like grains
of sand let trickle through an outstretched hand:
I need new words, a language that explains
without requiring me to understand.

Not Written in the Bodleian Library

(for a full list of the resources not consulted for this poem, see http://www.bodleian.ox.ac.uk/bodley)

Without a reader's card this library
is fortress: all its spires are barbed; its doors
dead nailed; unsmiling uniforms guard floors
of wealth that only the elect may see.
"But sir is free to browse through our gift shop."
Or sir may sit and stare at cliffs of stone
that rise like judgements of a petty god
refusing paradise to one poor sod
not even fit to be expelled, just shown
the gate at which he's welcome not to stop.

The stupid, the ill-bred, the dense, ill-starred,
the hoi polloi, the mob, the never-mourned
are milling, taking snaps in your courtyard,
and wondering. So don't say you weren't warned.

Old Undies

(your birthday poem)

My face is like old undies: the elastic
is gone. I crease like washing left too long,
too wet in the machine... and that faint pong...
old cheese, back of the fridge, still wrapped in plastic.
It isn't pretty and it comes to all.
I comfort my old papery skin with touch:
with wattle, feathers, dough, with turning pages,
and memories of thinking there were stages
of my life when something mattered much.
But luckily, my mind moves past recall.

When you have birthdays, you just look as though
your beauty is the nacre of the August skies,
and beauty only changes form to grow.
Each year I'm meant to think it no surprise.

Without your silver iteration

Without your silver iteration birds
provide my morning: waves of song are light
to light my bed with memory of words
I once heard whispered to me in the night.
Without your touch, your memory is all.
Without your perfume, toast and coffee fill
my kitchen with their scratchy linen folds,
the radio's a waiter: here's the bill;
a memory of hands another holds.
Without you, morning doesn't break; it falls.

My days are torch lit nights. I live in rooms
I recognise from brochures or suppose
I might if cognitive ingress resumes.
Without your knowledge, no one really knows.

Accompanists

Believe I think of you believing I
am also in your thoughts. Believe and know.
I take the melody you sang and go,
accompanying you until I die.
I hear that song each time my eyes are closed.
When you believe that you don't think of me,
believe me, you'll still hear the notes I play
and think you hear a pleasing lover say
his complement is you, and yours is he.
Our music plays forever uncomposed.

No final curtain. No applause to end
the set. No last, grand chord. No flowers.
My always ever only lover friend,
you are accompanied: all days, all hours.

My lover's lover's name

for Desdemona, lying

It tastes like foetal blood miscarried
through my mouth, an iron, acrid taste.
It smells like wreaths of flowering human waste,
of menses, menopause, of never married.
I roll that name around my mouth and dream,
in love with something ugly, fierce, and true,
addicted to its poison and its sting,
the snake bite pain of sharing not a thing
again with you, of keeping secret from you.
I mouth it in a long, slow, silent scream.

I wish you well: a deep and slimy hollow.
I wish you echoes: ten for every cry.
I wish you all the blackness you can swallow,
and knowledge of your drowning as you die.

Already last week's paper

Already last week's paper—so remote
but still familiar. Do you ever pause,
review, reflect, rethink effect and cause?
Do you re-read the letters that I wrote?
Or ball me into fists to light your fires?
I'd like to think you sometimes wear that ink
we spilt in newsprint, smearing words on skin,
a blurred tattoo without of what's within:
an old regret you never need to think.
No one can reconcile their past desires.

I hope I'm wrapped around the crockery
each time you move. Protecting something old
or commonplace. No doubt you'd call that mockery.
I saved you nothing then. Or so I'm told.

A Thousand Things

It must be spring. The pubs are turning into
sushi bars; old women into lanes.
You almost feel the tarmac throb as plane
trees warm their engines. Birds sing, or begin to.
A day, you'd say, that made a great page one.
But nothing starts. It follows. It's a script:
the weather, characters, the funny scenes
when you were younger, casting round for genes
to leave your offspring properly equipped—
but all you leave is all you've left undone.

It feels like spring. My father knows he's dying.
The room is full of flowers and not much else.
A thousand things undone—none now worth trying.
I wish the bloody flowers didn't smell.

I Contact

She lets me touch her honey skin. She calls
it I contact. I call it heroin.
The bathroom basin's full of soaking smalls,
as slippery as veins. I zero in,
and this is what I call success: success.
Her words are soft as floorboards on my spine,
unhinged as kitchen cupboards, wild as soap;
each touch a splintered sharp of Baltic pine,
each kiss the warm, wet, breathlessness of dope.
She says, "Two noes can make a kind of yes."

She lets me touch her. I contact, she calls it.
Her words are warm as something warm. I zero.
The cupboards, doors, the floorboards, walls, a bit
of something warm. A kind of yes. Eyes zero.

Fossil unremarked

Preserved in lines of sedimentary verse
my life is left a fossil no one's found,
still locked in rock and buried underground,
or weathered into dust the winds disperse.
I hope it blows your way. I hope you sneeze.
I lived in tropic jungle or beneath
a long dry sea, surrounded by those other
life forms that the sea mud failed to smother;
but I impressed vague tracks, odd bones, bad teeth:
a pointless preservation no one sees.

Most seeds will never seed; most fossils stay
entombed and never studied, polished, shown,
discussed, or argued over. That's okay.
The dark is comfortable. It's all I've known.

Winter morning

Whatever had to have been cannot be.
Smoke rises to the pearl grey sky and weaves
itself unseen. Whatever had come leaves
and leaves to 'dream' synonymous with 'see'.
You disappear like winter morning breath.
The cold rain falls like gravel hitting tin.
We wrap ourselves; we hide the selves in wool
and feathers, drawn inside the tidal pull
of womb warmth—let no heat out, no light in—
and make believe our body warmth cheats death.

I thought I saw you, walking with your friends.
You turned and smiled to them. Same smile.
Just different you. The winter morning ends
and leaves me nothing I can reconcile.

Sonnet 29

For thy sweet love remembered is a knife,
a swallowed razor blade or broken glass,
a jagged kidney stone I cannot pass;
your sweet love promises to end my life
and never does. It burns. Creates new scars.
I wear your decoration on my skin:
the random tattooed lines, the ugly brands,
a language no one but you understands,
an argument that no one else can win.
Your sweet love has the breath of abbatoirs.

The long walk up the hosed clean metal mesh
to killing floor. The Judas goat. The smell
of others' blood. The living turned to flesh.
And you. So this is what it's like in heaven.

Longitude

(the lowest orbit)

Around and round we go and never find
an edge to fall off. Longitude's a con:
you're warmer, hotter, cooler, colder—gone.
Each new location only part defined,
although you've done the latitude before.
I don't remember ever being here.
I don't remember waking, wishing you
had used the name of somebody I knew,
and feeling flat as rings of last night's beer.
Another day reveals another shore.

Time is position. Check your watch. Replace
the figures. Plot each spot you orbit: low,
but regular as any mass in space.
I might see you around... (And round we go.)

Woman with Creutzfeldt-Jakob Syndrome

You only know you've got it when your brain
starts turning these unnecessary tricks.
At first you pause and blink and look again
and try denial till at last it clicks:
you've got twelve months of madness left to live.
It could be worse. You've got more time to kill than
you might; so live the remnant to the max.
Try not to think about it while you still can.
Who needs a mind in order to relax?
Not even God needs reason to forgive.

I only wish my brain had been a jellyfish
to start with, drifting through the endless seas;
a scrap of living in a petrie dish,
unknowing any but its own disease.

God is my (only) judge

The rest are wasting time: your own (don't care)
and mine (do care). I make no statements now.
God knows already—doesn't need the how
and why, with whom, how often, when, or where.
Your prurience can prickle you with lust,
but don't expect that I will scratch that itch.
Don't come to me to hear a detailed list
of coital misdemeanours, things you missed,
of close to rabid mountings, dog meets bitch,
explosive penile boom and jubbly bust.

It's possible that nothing much occurred.
Again, don't look to me to tell you so.
Believe the almost certain lies you've heard
or not. I really couldn't care. Just go.

Ocean Blue

paint sniffing in Hawthorn 2005

Josh wears the woad of serial defeat
with nonchalance. He shows shy hands and laughs
and says, "It's prob'ly on my face as well."
It is. A small horizon that surrounds
his mouth and world. He says, "It's Ocean Blue."
Blue ocean on your postcard of a face.
Sweet boy. I wish you'd never travelled there.
I wish I heard your dreams without the smell
of solvent on your breath. What bastard mind
invented solvent for such vapid dreams?

Josh tells me he's an artist. Tells me blue
is infinite and everywhere—in space,
he tells me. Space. It isn't emptiness.
It isn't walled. It's everything. It's blue.

When words run out

(a visit to the nursing home)

When words run out, we look at pictures or
we find a sunny spot to sit and let
the birds converse of things we can't forget
until next time. We've lived most days before.
Each visit is more process than event.
At times, the rivers run, but times like these
the rivers dry, form sanctuary pools
where life recuperates as each day cools,
and words are sounds, leaf-murmurs in the breeze,
where life is nothing more than its intent.

Her bird-frail memory is never still:
a figure turns a corner, someone plays
that song, her sister Mary taken ill...
I fly. Birds roost. Words run out. No one stays.

My life in amber

Preserved as I was broken: wings awry;
my legs a spastic cross-hatching, a scrawl;
my abdomen and thorax curve: a small,
eternal question mark of pain. Dead fly.
You wear me on a chain around your neck.
I'm unaware in here of anything.
I don't know if you look at me for more
than any morning's careless making sure
of lipstick, blush, mascara, wedding ring;
the five sec. cursory perfection check.

You take me off at night. I'm not aware.
You place me on the table by your bed
and welcome this day's lover to his share.
Preserved as I was broken, like I said.

One last poem

Where are you now? Where do I send this last
of many? What's become of you/us/me?
I barely perched upon your family tree,
but still, I'd like to think that something's fast:
a memory, a sound, an incident.
Where are you now? I know. That cloudy place,
that place of mists, of postcards from a friend,
of work, of flowers no one thinks to send,
that place where mirrors hold a single face,
where wistful has the force of old intent.

Goodbye. The word 'last' always twists my gut,
but this is something last, the final must:
as fine as smoke, an end of thread that's cut
and curls and falls, a single cobweb, dust.

Death of sorts

Not being seventeen means suicide
is out. It seems I've lost the will to die,
but is this living? Have I found a lie
too powerful to ever be denied?
The vital signs are there, but life is not?
It could be that this breathing's not my breath—
perhaps some other creature puffs and gasps
and I'm the life preserver that it grasps
and uses while denying me my death.
That would explain why I don't feel so hot.

I'd like to take a tablet and lie still
and close my eyes and find that dark, blank rest.
If anything's alive and has the will
to keep me going—fine, and all the best.

The Botanic Gardens/ Sparrows/Ruth

Your footsteps scuffle down along the branches
and gather in the gutters against benches
or skip along the paths of your design,
a crazy clockwork that keeps only your time.
Your lawns are flexed like muscles under skin.
The water laps a tongue inside my mouth,
and fallen leaves, damp with your scent and taste,
are tensed in waiting and in waiting moist
for gates to close too late and let night in.

Each day will bring new picnic crumbs;
you'll taste the seed of many sowers' hands,
and leave into your leaves when nightfall comes
and lisps the words that no one understands.

Eleven minutes later

Eleven minutes later things had changed.
Copernicus' system was endorsed,
a whole new orthodoxy was enforced;
the galaxies of thought had rearranged.
Eleven minutes later, you're not here.
It takes ten minutes to destroy the world.
I now have first hand evidence of that:
my blue-green sphere squashed absolutely flat;
you float off smiling, boyed, as I sink, girled.
Eleven minutes: everything is clear.

Time keeps its bony grip on every wrist
and bores you with its tedious confusion;
its acrid breath, raw vodka with a twist,
drunk arguing its way to one conclusion.

Rain Check

In case it rains for twenty years or more,
keep this. You might need me to run a line
of kisses from your neck along your spine,
rub oil into your skin, unlock a door,
or lock it and let no one knocking through.
You might not. That's okay. No one insists
the future plots a course you must traverse.
You'll spin, you'll stray, you'll wander, you'll reverse—
your steps determine where your path exists.
I'm happy just to dance a step or two.

I wish you frenzy and sobriety.
I wish you sunshine, clouds, cicadas, birds,
and love, in all its strange variety.
Keep this and when you need to, hear these words.

Eternal Love, surprisingly

Eternal love is brief and hurts forever.
Avoid it if you feel like feeling like
you haven't been impaled upon a spike
to writhe for the amusement of whomever
has chanced to pass to loosen their applause.
I said I couldn't live without you but,
surprisingly, it turns out that I can—
more proof for you I'm not an honest man—
but doors can only open once they're shut
(and love survive so many metaphors).

Our love survives, surprisingly and winks
its tiny, diamond light from somewhere deep.
Love's left to other nights, and neither thinks
that dreams illuminate our unasleep.

First Generation Airbag

I don't know if it saved me or just failed
to kill me, but the airbag nailed with force,
like two hooves of a large and angry horse,
or love: I hunched, both cushioned and impaled.
The ribs will heal. The sternum should re-knit.
The car is written off. Just so much steel
and shattered plastic, bleeding toxic fumes
and coolant, radiating toxic plumes;
it's destined for the carmic ferrous wheel,
recycled into next year's model's bits.

The only thing that flashed before my eyes
was someone else's shiny, silver car
and one thought choking me, smoke and surprise:
I'm still alive and don't know where you are.

Here comes the son

(Happy birthday to me)

I know I'm heading where you've gone. I feel
the fingernails along my skin that raise
these welts, the stench of foetid breath that stays
inside my nose and lungs, the blade of steel
that's drawn across my back in slow incision.
I stop and stand in pools of sunlight now.
I wait and drink the warmth and give my thanks
and smile at fate and all its puerile pranks—
it's soggy spitballs bounce off anyhow—
serenity is making one decision.

Some time today someone will play the Beatles
('Happy Birthday' off the Double White).
I'll sing along, the way we all repeat
our comfort phrases: 'love you', 'ciao', 'good night'.

Whisky ago gone

Your absence has the sting of single malt
and yet I sip your presence in this glass,
the aromatic warmth my lips let pass
and welcome in a rolling somersault
that fills me: memories of body heat.
It's evening now and even now the birds
are open-beaked with heat, their wings held out
to catch the smallest breeze. They hop about
without a song, like me, without the words
to say without you I'm left incomplete.

The whisky disappears like whisky does.
Your perfume in the glass begins to dry.
My head is numbed with whisky's gentle buzz,
not puzzled where you are tonight, but why.

Mars replies to Venus

And Mars replies without words. Mars replies
with other weapons: lips and teeth and tongue,
and Venus gasps her words through lips kiss stung
and wet with him, "Don't talk to me of lies,
believe, and leave me nothing more to find."
And Mars is soaring red and flaming through
an ink black sky to find that evening star,
to find the brightest light, to be as Gods are,
to feel the spasm of the one of two,
to fight his way into the heart's own mind.

And to remain with her. His dream: conquest.
To fight is not to win. His mind is war.
To love is never to be found at rest,
and Venus smiles, and Venus will have more…

Priest, dying

Receive this tiny burden and believe
I tried with all the strength of being weak
to act according to the words I speak
and failed. The time is come and I will leave,
but no one left expected any more.
You've known for many years this life would stop.
You didn't know the when or how, but you
are not surprised, and you and me makes two:
at my age death is just a bubble pop,
the closing of a barely open door.

I want to say goodbye. I want to give
you something to remember; words so wise
that you'll recall them every day you live,
but all I've ever said is lies. All lies.

Refugees

for Julian Burnside

Australians all, we may as well rejoice
and issue some commemorative stamps
to celebrate the concentration camps
we hide in other countries. That's our choice:
ignore them. Concentrate on other things.
These are not people. These are human flotsam.
These self-ungirt who trust their lives to chance,
they choose to drift on tides of circumstance.
Don't sell us hard luck stories—"Thanks. We've got some."—
You can't blame us for others' sufferings.

Some women in our camps are sometimes raped.
Some children may self-harm. Some men have died.
But these were lives that global forces shaped.
We couldn't change a thing. Not if we tried.

Teach me to dance

Teach me to dance, sharp as a silhouette,
as smooth as birdsong, tireless as waves.
Teach me to set my steps between the staves
by second nature; so I can't forget.
Teach me to dance and I will find you there.
Vibration, shake me free. Release me as
the clouds release the rain; the fungus gills,
the spore. I want your death that never kills;
I want what every disembodied has:
the chance to dance and to become aware.

I hear your music when I close my eyes.
I feel the other bodies on the floor.
Alone, at night, I feel my body rise
and disassociate to you once more.

Spaceman

Had I returned and told the things I saw,
it's true, I might have earned a lasting fame,
but no one travels to return the same
and I am not the man I was before.
The other living worlds are hideous.
They pulse with molten life, obscene
with replication, stinking of decay.
I forced myself to witness them, not look away,
and now I pay the price for what I've seen.
There's nowhere that's not better rid of us.

The only beauty in the universe
is emptiness: the energy of matter
existing in its absence, its inverse,
the frozen moment time saw timeless shatter.

Love on stage

But this is not the time to think; this is
the time to act, to read the script and strike
the languid pose, or improvise and, like,
you know, make up the dialogue, the his
'n' hers, the cut and thrust, the loss and gain.
But this is not the time to think. To think
is to admit mistakes are sometimes made.
No one who thought was ever unafraid
and love's to fear as water is to sink:
what ever else, it's heading down the drain.

We'll be all right as soon as we're on stage,
positioned, waiting for the curtain rise.
We know our lines now better than the page.
It's fantasy. It's love. It's life. It's lies.

Blue dish cloth

(Suicide watch ward)

The weather is a Rubik's cube. Rain falls
and drips like dominoes. A Scrabble board
is folded and a stream of tiles is poured
like thunder when the conversation stalls.
The visitors make noise they think is thanks.
The smell of cabbage is a needle in
a vein, with dinner and departure comes
the ooze of medicated blood which numbs,
Spakfilla for the holes beneath your skin.
We wait for sleep to fire its useless blanks.

The hollow bounce of words on ping pong tables;
the tele bubbling like a fish tank, filled
with drowning creatures out of Aesop's fables.
Blue dish cloths wipe up anything that's spilled.

Let's all feel sorry for Les

Les says that he was fat, and I believe
what Les says. Les says childish taunts were hard
and left protective layers of blubber scarred:
someone like you, Les says, cannot conceive
the pain. Les feels it walking on the beach.
Les feels the insult spray, the mocking glance
of brown-skinned, slim-hipped, muscled, oiled, and buff—
the solar sting of their contempt enough
to hurt more than his soft sole/hot sand dance—
oh, to be cool! It's always out of reach.

Les missed the laughter, comradeship, the love…
but better for it: Les is become a name;
his words revenge him now; he's far above
beach scum (which leaves him pretty much the same…)

Fifth Wheel

The universe is full of wheels. Count five
and stop—of course you think the fifth wheel's you,
but keep on counting for an hour or two
and here's the reason you keep me alive:
you're one wheel in a million. One. The one.
We chase ourselves around the whole nine spheres
of heaven: comets, planets, moons, and stars,
and find ourselves alone in crowded bars.
You smile and every other disappears.
I wheel in orbits no one's ever done.

Your spinning sets the universe alight,
that whirl of sex and smiles and laughing: you.
A single star looks tiny in the night,
but light and love are all we have that's true.

The only man on Skype

You'd almost call me lonely if it wasn't
for the Echo / Sound Test Service... Hello
pretty English girl instructing me,
who lets me talk to her, records my words
as carefully as if she meant to tie
them with a ribbon, hide them tenderly
beneath her handkerchiefs, and re-discover
them in thirty years, remembering
the one, the one man who, in all those years,
responded in a way that she responded
to, the one whose message wasn't just
a testing, testing or a blah blah blah.
You almost call me, don't you? But you don't.
I'll never hear you tell me who you are.

Dags and Fat Kids

One day the news will break from Hollywood:
the team of dags and fat kids never wins—
the chiselled, handsome bastards are too good;
the weak might make a stand (and so might nine pins)
but true hearts only triumph in large frames.
They won't beat city hall, put on that show,
outbox the bullies, win the gorgeous stars;
they'll cower in the crossfire, die in snow,
be slain inglorious: the unknown extras.
There! Missing from the credits! Read their names.

They'll pay to watch their stories on the screen,
the orphans born without the royal mark,
enduring life, scene after dreary scene,
while spilling tears and popcorn in the dark.

The other judge

"... add faith, Add virtue, patience, temperance, add love, By name to come called Charity, the soul Of all the rest; then wilt thou not be loath To leave this Paradise, but shalt possess A paradise within thee, happier far." — lines found underlined in a copy of Milton's Paradise Lost

I spit on Charity. I spit on fools
who kiss defeat, who think my cause undone.
No paradise is lost—it's not yet won.
The one who sits in judgement sets the rules
and you will all, one day, be judged by me.
You worship the eternal you surmise,
but stone outwaits the moss; the rain, the stone.
You only see the world that you've been shown—
you clever things, you're in for a surprise
when I allow new worlds for you to see.

Tectonic isn't slow for all. I blink
in aeons. God himself taught me to wait.
The thing you worship isn't what you think,
and I have plans for you. I call them fate.

Then they expect you to pick a career

for Lizzie

Careers are over-rated. Set your sights
on something higher: worship God in ways
that don't require belief. Be one who prays
with kisses given/taken deep on nights
when stars fall, calling like small waves on sand.
Not everybody has a calling; so
be grateful you can hear a thousand voices;
delight in being unconfined by choices
that others use to write on labels. Know
that you will know life they won't understand.

You cannot make mistakes if you make joy.
The time is only yours that you have spent;
so spend up big and constantly. Employ
your life in living life. And fuck employment.

Another nothing

This is my work, and if it seems to you
a slight thing, an unnecessary thing,
a nothing, this thing needed me to bring
it into being. Its readers may be few,
but this I did. My work. My work and wage.
My friend says, "No more sonnets. Turn your hand
to something other people want to read."
He thinks I care. He thinks I have some need
for strangers to read this and understand.
I like the sound words make upon the page.

My friend says, "No more sonnets. Write some prose."
The swallows have returned; the wattle, too.
Why we repeat these cycles, no one knows,
but purposefully, we do what we do.

Poem in a moleskine journal

for Al

He photographs. I write. The same absurd
delusion, never more than half-believed,
the mild obsession of the self-deceived,
compels us to an image or a word,
arranged like plastic soldiers on the floor.
He makes the most of negatives. What's wrong
with that? They'll work. Enlarge them, print them, frame
the buggers, hang them on your walls and claim
you knew what you were doing all along—
as confident as when we played at war.

The line that separates a masterpiece
from snapshot is a line, and lines are crossed
a million times a day, and lines are tossed,
rewritten, lost... and positives increase.

Paolo's dream of Francesca in the second circle

We shelter in our bodies while the storm
contributes only to the paradise
of staring into liquid chocolate eyes.
We make imperfect bodies' perfect form.
God is your only judge. I wish us hell.
I wish us our eternity. I long
for storms to silence every other voice,
to sing our celebration of a choice
to live defiantly of right and wrong.
God might judge us, but I judge him as well.

Not even hell survives reality.
There are no storms for us. There is no kiss
that cracks the heavens with its blasphemy;
there's just the calm of this: this nothingness.

Finishing School

for Anna

For every nail their hammers tapped into
your flesh, for every hole they drilled, for each
new scar they raised to leave that strange tattoo,
give thanks. The only thing the stupid teach
is wisdom—beauty which they cannot see.
Consider birds and flowers (as someone said)—
they have to pass the same exams you do:
none. If you sing and wear your petals red
then God himself will ask no more of you—
so who's to ask for more? Not them. Not me.

It may be obvious; it's still worth saying:
"A game with stupid rules is not worth playing.
What's left is yours. What leaves with me is mine."
So leave. And turn the light on, Bruce. And SHINE.

Lily

(the astrophysicist's cat)

I wear a sympathy with night: I'm black.
I'm soft, sure-footed, certain. I appear.
I seep into the house when you're not here
and when you are. I'm never gone. I'm back.
Like all my kind I know what matters: dark;
it holds the universe together and
apart. It makes the space I occupy,
catspace, between the garden and the sky,
the space you study and can't understand.
Before your big bang came my single spark.

The astrophysicist concerns himself
with his cosmology—and I with mine.
There's room for both: his books upon the shelf;
my stars, like cats' eyes in the night, feline.

The Bequest

To people of Australia I bequeath
cicadas. Let them every summer bore
(or try) their one persistent thought in your
thick skulls, and fail. Then let them pack up, sheathe
their drill bit voices, and return next year.
I leave you also that peculiar smell
of asphalt softened in the summer heat,
and dusted with the fur/scale/feather/meat
of roadkill, confident you'll use it well.
And if you don't? Who cares? I won't be here.

Regretfully, I have to leave you while
you're still developing your reputation:
the world's most stupid, greedy, careless, vile,
self-satisfied, unthinking, lazy nation.

Summertown, Oxford

(everybody's got their heads bowed down)

The mail lands in the middle of the hall
and Oxford starts. The sky is Oxford blue
(that's cloudy grey to folks like me and you).
Step out. On cue, the rain begins to fall.
The dons are gone. The chavs and tourists swarm.
This place—I should have known before I came—
does not exist. It's there on Google maps
perhaps, but Oxford isn't real. It traps
you into thinking it's a place, the same
you dreamt of, but it's only there in form.

No postcards of the scaffolding appear,
just pictures of the spires. Don't inquire.
The answer isn't what you want to hear.
The answer's Oxford. I must be a liar.

A Vision of My Dying

(a visit to my dentist)

There is a state beyond pain when the mind
dissociates and every sense is wonder.
Masked figures hover, music, warmth—I'm going under—
no longer numb, no longer so inclined—
I'm rising like a trout into the light—
Forgive me. I have spent my days for nothing.
My mouth is gurgling like a winter's drain.
The talcum on gloved hands. I thought to gain...
What was it? Something. Surely there was something.
Receive me. Tell me everything's all right.

Is this the way you'll have me die? Like this?
Their busy hands as light as butterflies
that dip and feed... forgive me... but I miss
the point... appointments... watching how he dies...

Firkin's first space walk

The psych test shows I'm one of those they call
divergent thinkers. My movements here, in space
are beautiful; I'm Pina Bausch; I'm all
and nothing; solid fluid; human race.
And that's my craft: not floating, just not falling.
I'm not surrounded, I'm somehow immersed,
reflections on my visor I can't see;
I'm dancing for the last time and the first,
I'm solid, fluid, spastic, balanced: free.
The stars are bird song and the stars are calling.

I don't do checklists: tick. I guess that makes
my choice of occupation very odd:
a spaceman prone to first and last mistakes—
no lifelines and no anchors here, thank God.

London

(Permission to be ugly)

You may be ugly here: let out your belt.
Don't wash or shave. Don't brush your teeth or hair.
It's London, and it isn't going to care;
indifference so great it can't be felt.
This town is built on artefact and bone.
We crowd the streets and pavements, busses, tube:
the locals, buttoned up, eyes down, take strides,
map-flappers gosling shuffle after guides;
it's all the same for born-and-bred or newb:
eight million people, each one on their own.

The timeline's skyline changes by the yard,
and nothing dominates or lasts—no dome,
cucumber, tower, spire, clock, eye, shard—
all come and go. It's ugly. Welcome home.

Narcissus checks his mobile

He lies there, curled up like a moon; the moon—
the other mirror—Narcissus immobile,
planted. The light shines on his skin's meniscus
like the shadow of a petal, pollen on
a stamen, like the glance he never shares.
He's waiting for her call, the call he will
not answer pointedly, determinedly,
half knowing it's a call she will not make.
He lies. He's curled. He's white, immobile like
a painted moon, a shadow on the stairs.

Immobilized, his mind is free to ask,
a childhood dream of bottled wishes, one thing:
Oh genie of the ring, perform this task:
a reflex action, make her call me. Ring.

A snapshot of the day nothing extraordinary happened

It started just like every other day:
I woke without suspecting I might win
the lottery; I washed and didn't think
of ways to rid mankind of anything;
I ate my breakfast without word from God.
I caught the tram and nobody invaded.
My work was only boring in between
the tea breaks. Didn't win the Nobel prize
and met no other life forms going home.
No house on my side of the street was odd.

I thought I'd take a photograph which proved
the day had happened, but I couldn't spot
the difference when the lens cap was removed.
I think the auto focus must be shot.

The Rich and Hungry Still

Bonbeach, 1993

I spare a thought tonight for all the rich
and hungry still who stand in evening dress
in doorways, too detached to busk, too careless;
who beg without a cup and make no pitch
for charity they aren't aware exists.
Too smooth to walk upon a grubby shore,
they drink no wine from cardboard boxes, throw
no fish and chips scraps to the stars; don't know
the cry of thirty silver gulls for more;
don't know the night sea's many alchemists.

One day they find there's nothing more to buy;
their final horror: loss of appetite.
Not ever having lived, they cannot die:
they end. For these, I spare a thought tonight.

A visit to the Comic's Lounge

for Wendy

Each generation has to learn to say
    fuck on the stage and think it meaningful.
Each time it is, and those who know the trick
    should stick it out, remembering to clap
in all the pauses left there for applause.
We only learn the things we knew before,
    and only know we've lost them when we learn
them all again, and then, we don't recall
    quite how it was, but only that it wasn't
this—which shows we're making progress, yes?

I know a joke which goes like this: the sun
    comes up and lights the day and everyone,
expecting nothing else, goes into town
    and works until, that night, the sun goes down.

Australia

(a Bicentennial portrait)

Give us again our daily piece of toast;
the missus blowing kisses from the door
like bubbles. Darling Clementine. Before
we married she was beautiful almost,
and I was three parts lethargy, one trust.
A nation of small dreams, we only build
occasional weekenders in the air
and can't fly, can't spend any weekends there,
but prune the roses, keep the snails and slugs killed,
work slo-mo overtime to earn a crust.

Let's sort of celebrate with foreign tall
ships skulking through our ports. Each triple mast
with men aloft, a Calvary of small
time crims: the captives of a penal past.

Vacuum Clean

Is this condition possible? I thought
a vacuum had to be an empty space?
I shouldn't even get to see the face
that's hanging in my mirror. This place ought
to be as clean as mortuary steel,
but this is empty of another kind:
it's object full but purpose empty, clean
of reason, free of knowing what you mean,
the blank of having nothing on your mind,
the space of having nothing left to feel.

All words resolve to facial gestures here—
no air to give them shape enough to call.
The time has come when everything is clear—
so clear you can't see anything at all.

The sculptor's model remembers herself

NGV 2010

In his hands I was beautiful. He made
my body sunlight. He was hungry for
my form. He tasted me. He made me sure
that it was right that I should be displayed.
I never knew myself like that again.
My husband never liked it—couldn't bear
to think that it was me, that others saw
my body as it was, the one before
the marriage, kids, the daily wear and tear.
And he was right. He didn't have me then.

The thing I most remember is his hands:
the way he worked, the way he touched my skin.
My body was a moment in those hands.
He made me beautiful and I loved him.

Happy Endings

But don't you wish that God himself had thought
of happy endings? Hadn't left it all
to us and fairy tales? It seems a small
thing for a God to realize. He ought,
you'd think, to have that sort of thing well sussed.
But no. He gave us happy startings in
their place. Big deal. Free chips at the casino.
He knows the odds: you're going to lose. I mean, no
self-respecting punter thinks they'll win:
they're buying time until the final bust.

And so, we're buying time. I don't suppose
you'd like another drink? I've got the cash.
I know a little bar where no one goes.
It isn't far; it isn't cool; it isn't flash.

Zoo

The third day that the keepers haven't been.
Our cages now are barred and barbed with pain.
The smell of weak flesh travels like a stain
through air; meat needers rage to their obscene
desires of carnage: us. They scream with lust.
This is a place of frenzy, dream, and fear.
We look for shadows—will they come to feed
or to be fed? Left with our single need
it hardly matters which. Our fate is here,
among the faeces, dirty water, dust.

The night is falling faster than before.
The wings of night things taunt us, free to fly.
No lights patrol our pathways anymore.
We're caged but we are stalked and we will die.

A Personal Archaeology

I shaped my flints. I lived in caves as well.
I helped to leave them full of bones and art.
I knew the secrets no one has to tell
and learnt my kind's pre-history by heart.
    I worshipped if I didn't understand.
But now I cover everything in Glad Wrap
and put it in the fridge to keep it fresh.
My food pre-processed—can't tell meal from crap,
alive from dead, the spirit from the flesh.
    My god is tofu—cultured, smooth, and bland.

No eagle, ibis, sparrow, pardalote...
They live to prey, to harvest, forage, scrounge...
Acceptance steals its fingers down my throat
and leaves me eating Twisties in the lounge.

Leave Me

Leave me the knife you use to pare your fruit,
a memory as clear as stainless steel;
the way you flay the apple skin and suit
the slices to the plate. Leave me to feel
incision, blade and blood, its taste, its smell.
You take your haircut overseas to please
another. Use the hand that touched me. Use
the lips I kissed to smile while foreign breezes
lick the skin I still taste as you choose
dessert, rehearse the route to your hotel.

You'll write, of course (salvation of the dumb:
the written word), sing songs another wrote,
and I won't read or hear, but you will come
to me in intervals, between each note.

Zombie Diggers, Attack!

Anzac Day 2009

Rouse the lazy buggers from their bed!
We need them answering our endless call:
new generations want to see them fall
in mud, in grainy black and white, fall dead
and rise, like dawn, like tears in teenage eyes.
Oh they had guts all right, back then. They saw
their guts, exploded from torn bodies, wore
their insides out, died writhing, but died sure
that others came behind: there's always more.
The young are not our future: they're supplies.

Get up you lazy bastards! Up! No death
for you, no sleep, no quiet bird song, no
repose: resuscitation without breath.
We need you to enlist the next to go.

Bungee walking

I'm bungee walking round the streets. That line
I bought is pulling taut. I ought to sort
of pull up short, stop wishing that you thought
of me at all, of anything of mine.
The fall is all: last thing I'll ever see.
Goodbye. I've said it. But I meant to say
you brought me flight, a leap of faithlessness
into these concrete footpath rivers: mess
you'll leave for someone else to clean away.
I'll stay. A stain on someone's memory.

I can't complain. My footsteps on their beat
repeat the same old stuttering refrain:
your life's not over till you hit the street;
and home is any lane in which you're slain.

Hesitation Wounds

"Persons considering a suicide attempt, or trying out the weapon to ascertain its effectiveness, may first make shallow cuts, referred to as 'hesitation wounds' in the literature."
— Wikipedia

We carry hesitation wounds around,
the duelling scars, the challenges we fought
and didn't win, the glancing blows that caught
us unaware, felled us without a sound.
We didn't only hesitate. We lost.
Wounds heal, but past mistakes ache on and on,
and cobweb you in dusty lines of pain
traced on your body every night again
as memory remakes whatever's gone.
Experience is not a single cost.

I'll show you mine if you will show me yours.
I'll bend to kiss the scars upon your skin;
my lips and tongue will trace them, taste their cause,
and we who hesitate might have a win.

Phantom Limb

The dull ache of the missing part you know
cannot be hurting makes you turn; it makes
you look—you stretch a hand to touch—it takes
your breath and reason—where the fuck d' it go?
The place it ought to be in bed is cold.
Controlling movement of the phantom limb
is crucial: practice is the only course,
acceptance of your only partial loss,
acceptance of design disguised as whim,
accepting this is history foretold.

That isn't breeze, that gentle tug that caught
your hair, the thought that something touched or passed you.
I felt it, too. It's more than something thought.
It's physically impossible. It's true.

The Godless

for Chris Wallace-Crabbe

As worker states collapse, the socialist
repairs to Racecourse Road and buys Big Macs
because the wife's tired and the kids insist
they're starving and it gets them off our backs.
Who can we turn to when the fries are down?
All hells of mine are clean and lit with fluro's;
the damned are stuffed with soggy, sugared pap
by smiling imps. What's so amusing? Who knows...
They grin at spilt shakes, kids' chuck, each mishap—
disciples of the world's least funny clown.

If Poetry disturbs proceedings here
it's only for a take-away, to nod
in sympathy and wish hell happy new year,
before returning rapidly to God.

Postcard from Ghent

You'd think that no one ever went to Ghent.
"Where's that?" and "Why? What's there?" "Has anyone
gone anywhere in Belgium just for fun?"
My time and cash could both be better spent.
Futility and Ghent. It's quite a team.
It's easier to find an ATM
than find another penetrable vein;
they shrink like startled cephalopods and stain
my skin with inky bruises. Chasing them
is chasing you or any other dream.

The architecture's fine. The crowds are light.
My euros vanish, thin as morning mist.
The hotel staff are pointedly polite.
The chemicals disperse and we are kissed.

Nicking the Picasso

(strange alphabets)

The how is easy to explain, but dull;
the why's another matter. Rearrange
the thousand index cards that clog my skull
a thousand ways—it still seems just as strange,
    as epileptic as crime ever gets.
I puzzle like the wholly colour blind
confronting bland grey dots: we know
a pattern is revealed to other minds,
or sullenly accept it might be so;
    illiterates before strange alphabets.

I must have cubist motives; all intent
is just a tarot of a set of random shards.
Inspection only leads me to invent
unlikely readings that ignore the cards.

Dog Days

Each week another youless month goes past.
Days spill, cornflakes and milk across the floor—
no more domestic mess than those before,
one in a series, never first or last—
the dog comes, licks my calendar away.
Each day a line is scratched into the stone,
and if those lines were lined up, end-to-end,
no gaps, no curves, omissions, kinks, no bend,
that line would stretch from here to on my own.
The dog will have its walk and start the day.

The heat of summer brings the smell of tar,
the last cicadas drilling through my head,
and memories of you: the way you are
is always now the way you were instead.

Hampstead Heath

I flew to Hampstead Heath so I could lie
and watch the planes thread cloud-bead necklaces.
This is the season everybody says
you should experience before you die.
I lie and feel the inner spring unwind.
I didn't come to gnaw the dry, unmarrowed
soup bones of history, or come to look
for faint lines in the margins of a book,
or potted wisdom underlined and arrowed.
Experience was all I hoped to find.

And all I found was lying on the grass
and hearing birds I didn't recognise
explaining how grass grows, days pass,
spring comes and will be gone, and how love dies.

Postcard to my Dad

It isn't easy—neither of us being real:
me, pre-dead,
and you, so very post.
It isn't easy knowing what to write
on the address lines; what to tell you, anyway.
I'm still alive.
Still here,
immersed in transreality,
and sometimes—now and then—
I think of you and wonder if you thought of me.

I can't wish you were here, Dad—
you're not real—
but don't I wish I was.
Your son.

The deal was truth, absolute truth

(First casualty of love)

Some things are absolute and some are true.
Some things appear to vanish, then they float
back into view, like photos of a boat.
Some things are obsolete and some are new,
and some things are. Invisible and there.
The truth is just another wave-form, pulse,
an energy that moves our words around,
converts them into light and lyre sound,
to lovers' twenty questions: true or false;
to something felt approaching through the air.

The touch upon my skin is not the sun—
that's only half of it. The warmth I feel
is you, your touch, the something that you've done
with words, with truth, imaginary and real.

Returning Virgins

Returning virgins, each sunrise renews
our chastities and longings, each day brings
its unfamiliar news: our wedding rings
remain unworn, the surnames that we use
remain unchanged, our bed not yet selected.
Remaining virgins, each day's end reminds
us love is difficult but worth the pain;
a smear across the sky, the sunset stain
of blood and lymph and bodies, words, and minds,
of wounds we choose, of other lives rejected.

If you were here, of course, you're never here,
but if you were, we might have kissed; we might
have fought; we might have made a few things clear;
we might have lost two virgins to the night.

She seems now

She was an angel once—she didn't seem:
a face the sun would never shine upon,
a vision, packing up and being gone
as she chose to, as certain as a dream,
as maddening and futile as her kiss.
She was a mermaid once—an old tale told
to ever new belief: men chanced the main,
tore back her comfortless grey counterpane,
and found and fucked her, silver, sexless, cold.
I should have learnt something from all of this.

She was a trick of light and wave and mind,
a longing conscious thought could not dismiss;
she vanished with the moment she defined.
I should have learnt something from all of this.

HIV +

The moon, as dogged as an albatross,
is sweeping city streets again tonight
and missing nothing—not a crack that might
provide a hollow for dead leaves to doss.
Its search is touching everywhere at will.
You hear it, dry as static in the air:
a rustle in the garbage, teeth on bone;
its footsteps scraping tempered steel on stone;
the silver fingers playing through your hair;
its breath inside your lungs; the brittle chill.

Each pane of glass reflects that drowned man face.
The secrets nibbled from its lips have died
in many smaller mouths and left their trace:
a single, legion corpse on its own tide.

The river Derci

i.m. Jim Gardiner

The river Derci flows across our maps,
across the borders, splitting town and field—
its source and course forever unrevealed—
the only river in the world, perhaps.
Its humid delta is a marsh of change.
It overruns the gutters, floods the streets,
spills into gratings, bubbles up again
to pour from showerheads or fall as rain:
it seeps into the pores of all it meets
with one fast law: the world will re-arrange.

You think this is a journey you're beginning.
You'll navigate with oar or sail or pole,
until you tire of pointlessly Huck Finning
and wade ashore. And let the river roll.

Another of my funerals at Melbourne Uni

Who is it isn't moving there? Outside
our sunless lecture hall on Melbourne lawn
they're reading papers, talking, dreaming porn
or future novels, making rules that slide
between the guessed, the spoken, and the known.
We could be there to watch as each collects
and ponders, classifies, and reconciles
their butterflies of silences and smiles;
but we're in here and feeling intellect's
steel teeth crunch past the flesh and into bone.

I know who isn't moving, isn't quick.
I'm buried overground: the wooden suit.
I don't remember even feeling sick...
No flowers, by request, but please throw fruit.

Universal submission guidelines

Lie down, roll over, show your private parts,
and if you have a tail to wag, then shake it,
but if you can't think what to say, just fake it.
This is Australia. This is, like, The Arts;
stylish insubstance fills the shopping carts.
No one expects too much; so don't deliver
and then you're certain not to cause offence—
as great a crime in art as making sense—
your slice of cake might only be a sliver,
but taste the icing (where addiction starts).

All correspondents will be entered into:
so spread 'em. We're not gentle, but we're fast.
We know what's good for you; we've all been through,
if not you, someone like you, in the past.

Perigee moon, Cottesloe Beach, 2011

(The morning swim)

The biggest moon in eighteen years dissolves
in light and waves, as if it never went
its promised path: arc of the continent.
That's how it goes, the way the earth revolves.
It's six am. I ought to be asleep.
I stand to strip my jersey, feel the cold
brush sandy fingers round the waves of flab
that blanket anything resembling abs
and stand exposed: alone and pale and old.
There's only one way out of here: it's deep.

Your steps in ocean prove you're still alive:
they scarify; they rasp; they claw for red
mammalian warmth. You gasp, and clench, and dive,
and seek a moon among the white and dead.

First poem in ten years

(the fifty-fifty dance)

When you defined the rain as 'that which falls'
    it meant you only had to blame the weather
    for worlds imploding in your wake together—
your subtle perfume: dust, Chanel, and moth balls—
as you enjoyed the stillness of collapse.
But ruin isn't total; something moved
    beneath the rubble, something caught its breath,
    pushed out an axil, feeler, fed on death;
for something which had waited, life improved.
It flexes now: a spark across a synapse.

The brown light of the town hall shines on this truth:
    the tickets for the 50/50 dance
    sell out. Each second Saturday's a chance
to get right things age buggered up in youth.

Ikea Sappho

(the flat pack poet)

You check, and everything is there, which means
that logically, it will all fit together.
It must, because there is no Swedish whether.
Things work. Things run to time. Well oiled machines
and people. Both. They work. And poems, too.
You have your subject: classical, of course.
You have your well trained academic friends
to bend their hex keys to support your ends.
You're careful to make sure you note each source
(in case your readers aren't well-read as you).

And bingo! There you have it: poem. Done.
An hour's work, if that. You send it off.
You facebook friends: "It's just a bit of fun :)"
And they adore it! Oh! *embarrassed cough*

I wave at trains

Where am I left? I must sometimes appear:
the grey hair, blurred face, walking out of shot,
the accidental ambient. They've got
my image, even if it isn't clear;
I must be there, in someone's treasured snaps.
The long, slow ache to show that we exist
in any tense propels us and we go,
directed by no reason we can know,
aware of nothing that we've gained or missed,
but hoping time reveals something perhaps.

So, there I am the shadow in the background,
the motion blur where nothing clear remains,
the unknown, the connection never found:
a small child in a field. I wave at trains.

Behind the mirror

Behind the mirror, small, among the shoes,
beneath the jackets, dark, is space for me:
too cedar dark to be seen or to see—
invisible rescinds the need to choose.
I'm four and old enough to know to hide.
In here where space collapses on itself
the self itself collapses atom small,
a pinpoint in the nothing of the all,
a mote of dust upon an empty shelf.
The infinite is extant here, inside.

The now forgotten man, still wardrobe blind,
still-hearted still between each secret beat...
The airless dark extends to fill my mind
and hide me, and my hiding is complete.

The Rescue

You rescued me with that kiss, syrup sweet,
the vodka's sting, the suddenly connected
press of lips, the wholly unexpected
second kiss: the moment as eyes meet.
You rescued me and left me breathing, breathless.
Your smile is birdsong in the dark, it sings
of desert air, the silhouette of trees
against a dark horizon, evening breeze,
the smear of sun, of burning wood shavings.
Your smile persists beyond its time, deathless.

You made me leave you there. I turned to see
you smile a gentle, dark-eyed, farewell kiss.
You stayed, but something of you left with me,
and something stayed. It's something that I miss.

Nothing New (again)

This poem's ordinary. This is yours.
This one is yours to eat with square, white bread—
the one you don't remember having read.
It's white with none: effect without a cause.
It's ordinary, passé, dull. It's this.
This time is yours. Unspecial time. The day
when nothing happens, when the rain you were
expecting doesn't fall, when you're just her
and I'm the him with nothing much to say,
as passionless as any goodnight kiss.

The atoms that we choose to breathe have passed
through other lungs, through gills, through other pores
a million times as each thing breathed its last.
So this is nothing new. This one's all yours.

Cuneiform

Could anyone be bothered pressing these
in clay? Or scratching them in polished stone?
Words once were more than writing, were their own
accomplishment—you didn't read at ease,
you read at work, you dragged them from a field.
Then words were stooked, hand-tied, and lined in rows.
You harvested whatever you could carry.
But now, each day's another dictionary,
a library of untranslated prose.
We weigh the chaff and think we're talking yield.

I don't believe there's anything to say
that someone reading this in 3010
might think was truly worth the waste of clay
except, "I was alive like you. Back then."

Old news at the end of the pier

     They catch no fish and watch a grim bay dish
it out to cormorants and rocks. A fine
death waits at both ends of their fishing lines,
surprises them, and in they drop. The fish
won't bite. Men sink, white bellies up, in kelp.
     Unbated hookers troll the pier; sharp-eyed
as gulls they dodge the happy pairs and old
men used to stowing kit in other holds
to mob some teenage gobs who move to hide
their money and are lost. They smile for help.

"Had any luck?"—we toss our berley, sad
as Onan, on an unresponsive sea
and watch its sodden course—"Just bad..."
No angles. Just the great stupidity.

Kristine, because I lost the poems

Kristine, because I lost the poems and
the only villanelle I'll ever crack,
it seems as if I'm hiding you or planned
to slip your card from somewhere in the pack
to trump somebody. Someone you don't know.
I read about your Dad. I thought I'd write
but couldn't. I'm too distant now—my name
is not the one you used. One day I might.
I sound confused. You see I'm still the same
sweetwater buccaneer of long ago.

Kristine, I never understood past tense;
you are important to me now, again.
I'm sorry nothing that I write makes sense;
I'm happy now; I'm happy for the then.

Sex takes sabbatical

Sex took sabbatical when it was due;
she threw a few things in a cabin bag,
wrote 'No Address' upon the luggage tag,
found the departure gate and sauntered through.
When Sex decides to make a break, it's clean.
Sabbatical is not vacation. Sex
applied herself with passion to her tasks
to ask the questions no one ever asks,
and test assumptions no one ever checks.
Sex is a well-oiled, cerebral machine.

For those of us left standing at the gate,
who wave goodbye while praying for return,
it turns out love 's a long, hard wait—
the hardest lesson Sex would have me learn.

Four Swallows

for Lizzie, Anna, Katya, and Esther

    What fragment of a universal plan
is made apparent in those tiny heads?
What secret germ of knowledge do you spread
along the sinews of the flights that span
these senseless continents and endless seasons?
    Four swallows on a wire. Soon you'll be gone
to make your next impossible migration,
a search for one convincing destination
before the loss of will to travel on.
You have your purposes, if not your reasons.

Give my regards to anywhere you call.
Pass on a thought from one you chanced to meet:
The slave parts of this living whole are small,
unnumbered, unremembered, incomplete...

Time and Motion

She doesn't bother with the artful use
of psycho-casuistry. (She'll stroke her cat;
a man can stroke himself—you're proof of that.)
She says each action is its own excuse,
and shrugs, or squares her shoulders, almost sneers.
She only likes her lying warm and wordless:
two bodies on a bed. She softens then
and draws the strength out of her naked men,
creates some pattern, orders the absurd mess
of all their long-filed hopes and rankest fears.

She only offers that which men return;
not truth, not comfort, just a little time
and motion. Like or lump it, but you'll learn:
it's never you for whom the front door chimes.

Lamb

She says, The time comes when we all escape
the tyranny our hearts inflict on us.
Most manage with a minimum of fuss,
but you enjoy submitting to self-rape.
The rape as well, of course. You're doubly sick.
She calls that insight, but I understand
the disrespectful way I've come to treat
her; so I stand and listen to her bleat—
the rosemary and knife are both to hand—
when something's over, better that it's quick.

She watches unconcernedly and waits
to see who's getting less and who gets most.
It's Sunday night. I carve and load the plates.
There's nothing comforting about a roast.

It's Pez

She tips her head back when we kiss: it's Pez.
Dispensing sweetness through my mouth she says,
"I love the way you kiss; I love your lips."
My mouth is filled with sugar warmth; she slips
her honey tongue into my mouth; it's nectar,
it's blossom; it's a sudden shaft of light,
a dizziness, a need to hold on tight;
it's sea spray from the bow wave; it's the sting
of salt on skin, a transitory thing,
a butterfly, a butterfly collector.

I hear the fizzing in my head: it's Pez;
it's ice cream soda in a short glass—easy,
take it slow! She kisses me and says,
your 'thank you' sounds like someone saying 'please me'.

Cutlery Drawer

Let's spoon. Let's fork. Let's never, ever knife.
Let's lick our lips and kiss and hold each other,
stay warm and dark in bed and draw the covers
and cover morning—let's snooze button life
and only wake to find our dream in bed.
You had a glass of wine with someone else.
I heard about it in my lower gut.
You told me that you had to tell me but
you didn't have to and you did. As hells
go, there are plenty worse, it must be said.

Spoon: lying front to back and touching hips.
Fork: face to face, as fingers, legs entwine.
Fork: taken in your mouth, against your lips.
Spoon: supping you like broth. Fork spoon. You're mine.

The differences between me and Shakespeare

Well, one of us is widely read, of course.
And one of us gave birth to lots of words—
midwordery as I call it—and herds
of phrases and expressions still in force.
And one did not. No prize for guessing which.
Apart from that and other superficial
differences there's not a lot between us.
Comparisons aren't helpful and demean us;
so read between our lines—all art is interstitial—
accept that we both scratched a common itch.

Each day a thousand scholars probe and peek
and try to plumb old depths, but you are quite
alone. You read these words. You are unique:
the one for whom we both once chose to write.

First Dive

The sky is filled unhurriedly with cloud,
a mass, white-backed, breasts brushed soft gull wing grey,
and thoughts, too indistinct for words to say
amass, float, tumble, never form aloud.
The wind and sea contend. The white caps roll.
The sand is still warm here, protected by
the lee of tea treed dunes. Warmth radiates,
a source that strokes and penetrates,
and leaves you one with sand, with where you lie.
You're filled with life beyond life you control.

To stand, to walk into the sea, to gasp
as cold salt water stings the sun from skin,
to dive, to let the waves and water rasp
your mind to clarity, is to begin.

The Lost and Con (ten lines of eulogy; four lines of prayer)

i.m. Vicki Bartlett

Lost and confounded; behind the ifs and buts,
the oldest thug: mortality; its flecks
of spittle on my face; knee in my nuts;
the simple ache beneath our every complex—
the key you feel unwinding in your back.
We gather here to celebrate and mourn
someone who never had a snowflake's chance.
Like all of us, she happened to be born,
was pitched into this spastic, clockwork dance,
and fought to keep her feet through every track.

Don't make me sing a hymn. Don't make me pray
and look for God among the black shoe laces.
When no one here has any more to say,
I'll go. Don't let me see her children's faces.

Prayer at a bus stop

Don't let me die. Not here. Not where I've spent
so many hours of intent in stasis.

The basis of my faith is waiting here,
expecting something to appear and take me,

accept me, shake me, move me to a new
pitch, somewhere with a view, a clear view—not this—

not dying here, my money in my hand.
I planned a different trip today. I had

a dream to get away. I had the means
of getting there: as dreams go, pretty small.

Was that the problem, after all? My bum
is sore. The bus will come and I will go.

I know the choice I have is to believe
or not. Don't let me die here. Let me leave.

The Estate

I occupy the park bench long enough
to feed the sea gulls half my bloody lunch.
They know precisely by some gastric hunch
when it runs out, and when it does, they're off.
They're birds with little use for sentiment.
This moment, my estate is only that
my broad arse covers. What of intellect?
What gems of mine can any recollect?
The half thoughts mumbled, scribbled, shouted, spat;
the words I used which weren't quite what I meant.

I stood; I fell; I cried and sucked my thumbs;
I tried to learn my tables; did my sums;
I married; worked; I wiped up tiny bums;
and after sea gulls, sparrows search for crumbs.

Before the visit to Mad Aunt P.

Your Auntie Pauline has a Lego set,
    collected over years. She only buys
    the white blocks and insists they're all one size.
She files the bumps off so you kids don't get
ideas. So don't get any. Just sit tight.
We've never known what makes your auntie tick.
    Despite what neighbours say, she's not unkind—
    it's true when they call round she draws the blind—
but she's the one who suffers, poor old stick.
We'll leave, but she's stuck there, night after night.

Disclaimer: Politics is more than show biz.
    It's not a joke, therefore I state: One Nation
is copyright, P. Hanson. Lego is
    a trademark of the Lego Corporation.

Beograd explained with kajsijevaca

(Warning: some of the nuances of a long evening's splav conversation may not have been captured in the following fourteen lines.)

It isn't Paris and it isn't Prague.
It isn't beautiful. Nobody, you
don't fall in love with Belgrade, you just curse
its stupidness, its nothing making sense,
until, one day, you find you haven't left.
One day you find yourself explaining it
to someone just like you, confused because
the bars, the restaurants, the clubs aren't better
but they're here. And nowhere else is here
because they don't know Belgrade. No one does.

Do you use whores? It's not a whore. Belgrade
would starve! New York, Berlin, they'd do all right,
but we could sell it free and not get laid.
But we'd be out there—working—every night.

Tow Truck

I'm parked. I close my eyes. I wait. It's coming.
Rain oxidising steel, a cruciform,
two roads, one intersection, coming storm,
the wires in the skies are really humming.
I smell the diesel rainbowed on the tar.
The glow of dashboard lights, the radio,
the memories of nights spent waiting for
a big show, slumped against the cabin door,
the ambo, towie, cop unholy trio,
backstage, we wait for screams, we wait to star.

The headlights coalesce and curdle, pass;
another set of heartbeats I forget.
Tonight, no television lights, no glass,
no blood, no flame, no singing flesh. Not yet.

The mathematics of your legs

Your legs eleven
next to mine
eleven plus eleven
twenty two that's two ducks swimming
quack quack
two legs two legs
two plus two
is two squared
two is one and one (eleven)
your legs eleven squared is 121
your leg my legs your leg
quack
one two one
I love the mathematics of your legs

Christmas Adam

It's Christmas Eve and everything is shut
except the hole you left. A hole in space.
A hole you're choosing not to occupy
and I'm as scared of you as light is of
its prism. I see you and dissociate;
I shatter into rainbows, make a spectrum
of myself... your wake is human tinsel.
To everything a season: time to shop,
a time to deaden pain, a time to cut
and run. You've got to go. I've got to stop.

The only thing I change is where you're not
and introduce your absence through the streets.
Occasional late shoppers flash past—spots
of neon in the darkness they complete.

Other men

The other men will catch the spiders in
their kitchens, wrestle jar tops, change the light
bulbs, check the funny noises in the night
and, nervous, stub their toes and swear and win
their kiss when stomping bravely back to bed.
My thanks to you. The role may be a lead;
it's not heroic: it's a soapie, it's
a typecast grind. You'll live in catch phrase bits
of script you once believed you'd never read.
You won't believe the words you'll find you've said.

Night comes to everyone alike. It's dim,
not dark. It's not as scary as it seems.
When night comes, there's a hum of every him,
of prayers for love, for sleep, for change, for dreams.

1000W Smile

Incinerate me. Turn it on me. Let
me feel my skin heat, then begin to burn
beneath your searchlight smile. I want to learn
I can't resist your questions. Better yet,
just tell me what you want me to confess.
I can't deny you anything—you're so
fist to the solar plexus beautiful.
Alight with pain, I'll try to play it cool,
but you'll decide, you'll tell me when to go,
and leave me here, a charred and crumpled mess.

You nominate the time and place and crime
and I'll commit it. Anything to please.
Just tell me what you want, just say that I'm
the one for whom you'll throw away the keys.

Full stop

I want to set the final full stop—pop!—
right here. I want to tie a ribbon round
the lot. Let not another line be found.
I want this tedious pretence to stop.
I've written all I can. I need to heal.
So many full moons shine their way into
my front room; same old eyebrow raised as though
it had some knowledge that I'd never know.
Old fraud. As if it cared any more than you,
as if it could be bothered how I feel.

A nightly possum rattles through the trees
and at my window, peers and disappears.
It's made blurred possum sense of what it sees,
the secretless, unmeaning sounds it hears.

Discovering the mirror

Is this what separates us? Have I found
the mirror plane and not your finger tips?
If I lean forward will I touch your lips,
and if they move with words, will I hear sound
and feel your breath, or only see it mist?
The lights came on. I thought I saw another—
another room, another person's mess;
but now you say it's simple onliness
of husband/wife, man/woman, father/mother,
and onliness is why we've never kissed.

If I can't touch you in the light, we'll meet
in darkness when we meet within the plane.
However briefly, we can be complete,
until the lights are switched on once again.

Ukraine 2022

The mothers ask their simple question: why
did I give birth? Why did the life I formed
and cherished, taught, protected, nourished, warmed,
why did I make life just to see it die?
Their fruitless questions asked of a barren God.
Destruction is the moron's only talent.
To bomb, to sack, tear down, to make life cease,
to take a razor to a masterpiece
requires mere submission to intent—
the free will granted any arthropod.

Men are the agents of their own decay,
an infestation, plague, disease of state.
We are our own inevitable fate,
the something rotten, eaten, mouldering away.

Tripwire Town

Don't have to drink to stumble down this street;
you trip me up, you stick a cane between
my legs. I fall for you, again I'm seen
on hands and knees where blood and pavement meet.
You leave me as you found me: on my knees.
The need for chemistry. I'm in a hurry.
I choose the camouflage of booze to blur
the outlines, bodies, him and her,
and beat my boxer's brain into a slurry
and suddenly, I'm not too hard to please.

I leave the safety of the bar too soon.
The hard men mill around, parade their scars.
I look away and look up as the moon
gobs in my face its spittle spray of stars.

I miss the you

I miss the ideal that I made of you.
The fault all mine, I know, but if I made
too much of the perfections you displayed,
assuming they could possibly be true,
I didn't get it altogether wrong.
You were as beautiful as bees, your voice
that thrummed its wingbeat accents through my head,
and promised me the honey that you fed
to someone else (yes, fair enough: your choice)
your voice was one continuous love song.

I miss the smoky walk towards your hive.
I miss you on my skin. I miss your sting.
I miss the buzz of knowing I'm alive
to hear each syllable your voice lets sing.

Blank white man

You have the letters, several alphabets
and languages; so what can I bring you?
A plot? A character with flaws who rings you?
Someone who says and does and then forgets:
a something blank and white to write upon?
I am your clay. I'm dizzy on your wheel.
I'm canvas, blank and primed, my surface calls.
I'm stony cold until your chisel falls
and hacks me, carves me into something real.
Cicada song by day, by night, I'm gone.

I'm embered in your love; I glow in you,
remembered, real, still warm, and always still.
Breathe on me, oxygen and lips, blow through
and fire me, create, ignite my will.

Her body sprinkles adjectives

Her body sprinkles adjectives behind
her as she walks. I sweep them into piles
and try to classify them. She just smiles
and tells me not to pay them any mind,
but that won't work; I think we all agree.
I ought to write but don't. The things I want
to say are not the things that words are used
for. I need feathers, petals, things infused
with scent and touch, I need a sensory font
to show her body crushing and suffusing me.

And all I have is adjectives. I paste
them in a scrapbook, cautious, dutiful,
and wonder at their feeble glow, the waste
of words and breath, and she so beautiful.

The Unmapped Hamlet

The statuary was only ever made
of plaster in my garden and you turned
the sprinklers on. You watched it, unconcerned,
dissolving in a sodden, white cascade,
    and shrugged and said, "It would have rained one day."
Is this what happens when you haven't found
new Romes to sack? You march to any village,
invite your mates to join the party, pillage,
and raze an unmapped hamlet to the ground?
    No mouse should die a lioness' prey.

At least I now know how career vandals
    spend their leisure hours: practising.
You let your victims burn like birthday candles
    for just as long as your admirers sing.

A prayer for George Pell

Dear God, please let there be at least a type
of hell for Pell to show that you revile
this man of cant, of sanctimonious tripe,
this shield of pervert priest and paedophile.
Equip hell with a large Pell toasting fork.
Dress George like any other fatted beast
and slowly sweat the fat through glistening pores.
Let flames kiss flesh, persistent as a priest,
and scarify his hide with razored claws.
Fill caverns with the smell of roasting pork.

Please find a corner of eternity
where George can count the aeons as he learns
the pain of those betrayed, and may you be
as patient as a stone as George Pell burns.

I lived for art

I lived for art and died art-broken, Callas,
cold, unfeeling now. Vissi d'arte,
I heard with sobbing ears and learnt, in part,
that art is first a walk-on part in Dallas,
then Bay Watch, then, like waves, the credits roll.
I died and didn't go to heaven; I've
stayed here and watched as others came and went,
tried getting even as their breath was spent
as meanly as their money and their lives.
Will no one dig me out to leave this whole?

My prayers are sung internally. My walls
are hung with pictures, back to front. My phone
responds to bingo numbers no one calls.
It's not bad dead; it's horrible alone.

Another Way

(The Scenic Route)

The getting lost is easy, even after
the route is shown. The town has many paths
past flowering chestnuts, beeches, elders, ash,
that look the same to strangers, that lead to here:
you're lost, and all you know is where you're not.
That's why the scenic route's so good: you can't
be aimless when your destination's still
a blank. You have to keep on going. If
there was another way, I wouldn't take it.

And this is my repayment: not a thing.
I walked a dozen tree-lined tracks for you,
remembering how you were once and I
am now: lost somewhere on a scenic route.

Paralysis

Paralysis is still the teddy bear
I cuddle, huddled in the urined sheets
of night, night featureless where comfort meets
its absence, thought meets terror, love despair,
where logic leads to step-by-step confusion.
I think of you and her and her and me:
the pronoun tangle of comparative
analysis, the shattered narrative
of lives lived in their odd asymmetry.
I think of you and come to no conclusion.

Paralysis cannot conclude, instead
its slow hyphae expand and clog the brain
and build a mass congealing as it spreads,
as slow as fungus but as sure as pain.

Meeting John in Lygon Street

for J.P. & the M.M.T.B.

Not much worth ending ever finished at
the slamming of a front door, did it, brother?
Pretending otherwise is proof of that.
However distant, we're joined, each to other;
the sure electric traction of the past.
I think of shabby offices and jokes,
of anarchy that had a payday, a crowd
of students synchronising watches, smokes
in pubs, confessions, secrets shared aloud,
of transitory times that thought lets last.

It's never a mistake when couples split,
you said—and I can't argue, your once friend
who keeps your letters, still admires their wit,
who holds that friendship lasts beyond its end.

Sunset on two trees in different gardens

Her conifers are military trees.
They live and reproduce in rank and file
and wear their deep, drab military green
because it has a purpose, not a style.
      They live for close inspection on parade.
The ghost gum is possessed of different spirits.
It's undirected. Solitary. There.
Its limbs shaped to a chaos they inherit
from each day's growth into the flint hard air.
      He sits beneath it; sips the tea he made.

And who knows what goes on beneath the soil?
And who can say whose nourishment is drawn
from whose decay? And who decides it's worth
the wait in darkness for the chance of dawn?

Sugar muse

So sugar muse me, make me take it on
the lips, insist I watch, don't touch, and learn
to take instruction. Give me sugar burn,
those tiny crystals on my tongue… are gone.
Your smile explains why pain is sometimes sweet.
I want to see that honey flesh made real
beneath my fingers, tasted on my lips.
I want to lap in tiny, syruped sips,
and being tasted taste you as I feel
you salt me with the sugar of defeat.

I know this game's rules: look, but only touch
as circumstance allows and muse permits.
The muse will choose to spoon as little/much
as sweetens her before she calls it quits.

You only use those legs

You only use those legs to walk, but I
use them to carry me from A to Being
somewhere you are curled up on a bed,
to somewhere you are shaking off your jeans,
to somewhere you are sunning on a beach.
I need those legs to get me through each day
when traffic flows, the postie comes, the trees
surrender leaves, the phone submits to its
desertion and is filled with other voices:
as days without you stumble out of reach.

My heart sounds like your gumboots plashing through
mud puddles. Trample me. Go on, have fun!
Land on me with those legs, but as you do,
remember I will need them when you're done.

Cat

As I'm incapable of love, instead,
I offer that which seems to work as well:
a something you can love, a kiss and tell,
a something always warm to warm your bed.
And if that's not enough, then love me more.
You know that I am faithful in receipt
of love. However constant, vast your need,
know its enormousness cannot exceed
my appetite. I cannot be replete.
I am the perfect lover on that score.

Enough of talk. It's getting late and we
should head to bed. Do what you need to do.
Come gently, softly, don't unsettle me.
Bring warmth and I'll accept your warmth from you.

Predictive Text

It knows the words it thinks I should have sent.
I know the letter/number combination
that should unlock our fitful conversation:
it's never close to what I thought I meant.
Technology has left me dumb, thumb-tied.
So read the words I never send: I ache
for you, who's reading something else, the one
who smiles at things I haven't done,
remembering the calls I didn't make,
the sweet, romantic gestures never tried.

You know my words. You know the things I say.
You know my moves. You know the things I do.
I'm more predictable than yesterday.
I still can't find the words to say to you.

Does anyone know I'm alive?

The day assumes an eeriness, the light
dims, drops a watt or two, the colours flatten,
sky stains like water spilt on dirty satin,
and I wait for my one thought to ignite:
Does anybody know that I'm alive?
The birds excite the air. The trees respond
to wind. Call and response. All matter finds
its purpose colouring within the lines.
Why did I think I'd get to live beyond
the means to any end and still arrive?

Where everybody else has got a beat,
I've got a number. And it's running out.
I start to count the footfalls on the street.
I start to wonder what this poem's about.

Cathedral of Venus

(the smell of nothing)

It's rubble now. The thousands of our hours,
our carving, painting, setting glass—a slew
of rubbish for the peasants to pick through,
and steal the shards of treasury once ours,
once raised and dedicated to our God.
Odd remnants of the walls still stand and trace
our grand design, our folly, our supreme
co-work, the realising of that dream
that tortures and sustains the whole, sad race;
it's rubble now, and turning into sod.

Sod all. The all that's always left us: nought,
the nothing, zero, cipher, zip, the blank,
the everything that we were ever taught
or learnt. Who ever guessed that nothing stank?

The Serial Farewell

for Esther and Katya

Another day of our farewell. A process
much longer than a length of words can reach.
There's nothing I have learned that you won't teach
yourselves as you grow up and I grow less:
a waving figure trapped in your perspective.
Goodbye, my darling girls, goodbye. That's me
left on my platform mouthing words that pass
for sensible advice through dirty glass
as you feel those first pulses of your journey,
and see your faces over mine, reflective.

We'll keep in touch—exchange remembered lies
like snapshots taken only when the sun shone:
your Dad, a man I wouldn't recognise,
and you two on each point of being gone.

The Sugar Generation

We drown in Golden Syrup, amber goo;
in sticky pots of liquid fly paper
we dip our spoons and knives, our fingers, too;
as thick as porridge, nourishing as vapour—
the sweet, warm rush of empty kilojoules.
We know that nothing can go wrong, embraced
in honey folds of something that's almost
like teenage love (without the after-taste);
we smell as fresh as morning's buttered toast;
we shine like molten toffee as it cools.

You wouldn't call this living—this is better—
the sugar generation knows its fate:
we're going to die, so let's die someone's debtor—
they'll clear the table when we've licked the plate.

Woman in burqua

"Deception is the cloth, the cloak I wear,
my burqa, liberation in concealing.
My words are my chador to mask my feeling,
protecting me from him, his eyes, his stare."
She says she chooses to compose her self
herself, and doesn't want her him involved.
In isolation: contemplation, proof
of gods that flit beneath the temple roof
like swallows, divination, problems solved,
or, if not solved, placed on a higher shelf.

"It's dark. It may be my returning to
the mother womb—it's dark and warm enough.
It's where I process thoughts concerning you;
it's where I hide life's treasure from its stuff."

Anywhere but here

You can't be serious. I haven't got
another vein to open. This place smells
of blood and semen now, but something tells
me you expected that. Well, that's your lot.
You wanted blood. You got it. But that's all.
I never promised not to leave a mess.
I never promised to exsanguinate
to schedule, by such and such a date;
I only promised you complete success:
you're free of me. I'll never write or call.

I'm somewhere warm and wet and crimson. How
'bout you? I'm somewhere where the steam licks heat
into and from my skin. I'm floating now.
I'm anywhere but here. Let's never meet.

She Never Flips

She'll never have to see bits missing from
her jigsaw if she only rattles the box.
She's past help. Keys turn one way; nothing unlocks.
There's room for one voice on her intercom—
that's why she never flips the switch from 'Speak'.
Reality has talents it conceals
from everyone but her. When something snaps
(her fingers or her mind) our pasts collapse
and reassemble in a form she feels
is better suited to events this week.

Some little girls have magic things they hide
in pretty boxes, tucked away from view.
As long as no one ever looks inside,
the magic never has to be untrue.

The falconer

The falconer removes the hood: a simple move
balletic in its meaning: you are free
to dance the skies, to soar, to prey, to be,
to test the other cloud-soft lives, to prove
your being worthy of their blood, your air.
Each bird will take a moment to adjust,
a moment more before it leaves the glove
and trusts its eyes, its teacher, and its love,
and flies. But falcons do, because they must.
The hood is off the moment it's not there.

It's time to sally forth. Fare well, but take
advice: the view is better from cloud high.
Good falconers do not make a mistake:
a bird may not return, but all birds fly.

Because I woke up early

Because I woke up early, I went walking,
elbowed by the wind like surly crowds
that weren't there on the patterned stones of Lund.

The patterned stones of Lund arrange themselves
in semblances of meaning: mica, quartz,
and feldspar punctuate its cobbled grammar.

Grammar. What big Is you have. And what
big Noes. And what a toothless, stinking, shag
pile, matted dog hair rug you turn out being.

You turn out being somewhere near the burnt
stone church of Lund; stained charcoal with the smoke
of something very cold, of something Nordic,
something no one talks about in church.
I only saw because I woke up early.

When I could fly

When I was younger and could fly by just
extending wings and making that plane noise,
I wasted time in shooting other boys,
or crashing in the chalky playground dust:
no thought the day would come I'd not know how.
When I was younger and the treasure maps
were clear and clearly marked with X the place
you had to dig, how many steps to pace,
I left more booty in the ground perhaps
than might seem wise. I need those doubloons now.

When I am older and remembering
how beautiful you were and how I tried
to keep you, how I threw away your ring,
I'll wish that I was younger and had died.

Perfect black dress

The perfect black dress is—does nothing more
than call to form a body in your mind
with various perfections that you'll find
when perfect black dress falls and hits the floor.
It doesn't promise; it delivers sex.
The premise is a simple one: a sheath
of black to trick the longer look, the glance
of eyes across the body's lines, the dance
of vision seeking vision underneath.
Simplicity turns out to be complex.

What isn't hidden, no one seeks to find;
for women, black's the camouflage of choice.
Perfection is a state of body, mind,
and one black dress. Accept it and rejoice.

The Schwebebahn By Night

Around the neon-lit advertisements
the fattest spiders spin their careless webs
    Beside the ticket punch a couple
    and soft and spreading clouds of Turkish...
The river rises through the metal grille
a quiet static unheard in the city
    A derro touched me by die Brünnen
    for five Marks worth of there but for the...
Eine, die Hörzu zu Hause hat is peeling
away and waving well rehearsed farewells
    A gnädige Frau sits pucker faced
    and everyone's forgotten The Party...
The platform shivers—one way or another
the Schwebebahn is coming—someone's coughing

When you understand

It might be sanskrit, or a whisper heard
at night, an unknown shorthand, morse, a code.
You might have made it meaningless as birdsong;
it might be rain, or tyres on the road.
Why don't you tell me when you understand?
It might be many things or one near truth;
it might tick like a bomb, hiss like the surf.
If only I could face you and the proof
of lovers decomposing into earth,
accepting it as what you always planned.

You wave, and leave me here to sort through drawers
for patterns left by sea-gulls in the sand,
for sounds between the breakers and their pause,
for anything to touch I understand.

And as you age

And as you age and gather adjectives
and purpose weathers to its random form,
to something unconcerned with that which lives,
as fierce as dew, forgiving as a storm,
remember not to think of me at all.
I won't remember you and how I miss
and missed you all those missing years,
and finally together, we won't kiss
and be apart forever. No one hears
and no one hurts at no one's call.

You wouldn't recognize me now. I've gone—
become reflection in an ink black plane—
but I'll know you, each time you breathe, I'll know,
and you'll know me in every age again.

Oxford Physic Garden

planted 1621

The same herbs that cured nothing then are still
grown here and still cure nothing. Take your pain
around the garden beds and look in vain.
The diagnosis that I'm staying ill
is tart as stolen berries in my mouth.
I bob between the fresh grave beds. I read
the labels, mispronounce the Latin words.
I'm lost. I can't identify the birds
or flowers here. I'm foreign as a weed.
Physician heal me: plant me facing south.

I tear a bay leaf from its tree and crush
its brittle green, release its spice, and let
its perfume drug me with the poisoned rush
of memory. To heal is to forget.

When other people die

When other people die, I try to hide
the tee hee hee not me, not yet, and set
my face to 7. Serious Regret,
(I'd dial it higher if a loved one died)
and hunker down to wait the weeping out.
No doubt this coldness makes me seem extreme
in my self-centred beingness, but I've
observed a truth: they're dead and I'm alive;
so, too bad, deadies! Life may be a dream
but you're not in it, whatever it's about.

So tell me that I'm cold and unforgiving.
I'm not a man of whom it will be said,
"He left the world the better for his living."
I'll leave the world the way we all will—dead.

25th December at the home

There's nothing for the kitchen or the car
these days; the gifts are small and edible.
They stay just long enough to um and ah
their news and make excuses credible.
Somebody makes you wear a paper hat.
You're served your Christmas tea. You eat and doze
until the cheery girl comes for the tray
and chats while stacking crockery—"Were those
your grandkids? Yeah? Came all that way?"
insisting that you must have enjoyed that.

Some things cannot be changed: the television
(it's kept on channel Nine), mortality,
the past, house rules (to save you from decision),
your presence underneath the Christmas tree.

Sonnet for a superfluous man

Accept for fourteen lines the proposition:
you don't exist. It clarifies a few
things, brings your likely future state in view,
explains your strange, untenable condition:
the more you do, the less effect you make.
You speculate, but don't know what was meant,
a migratory bird who turned up late
and thinking it was early, chose to wait—
you'll winter where the snow sets like cement;
your path now clear—the one you will not take.

Not ending as you don't begin: not son,
not father, wholly ghost; you see
time stand, twin mirrors either side of one
point in a line of blank infinity.

Her cat is called Ulysses

for Ales and Gabrielle

Ulysses dogs us down the night soil lane,
   through paling forests, splintering with pique,
   his collar sounds like bellbirds near a creek
that sounds like water running down a drain.
We thought we knew where this was going to end:
a plan we had the foresight to forget.
   She stops to feel the bluestone. "Smooth," she says,
   a purring question mark between her legs,
"as mountain river stones," her fingers wet,
her body curling like a river bend.

We're not romantic. We know where we are.
   We don't say things we haven't said before.
The sound of breakers is a passing car.
   We know this is a footpath, no foreshore.

A first cartographer remembers his lost love in her bath

The line your skin makes breaking water marks
the outline of an unknown continent:
its mountains, castellated battlements;
its sea-lapped forest, strange and thick and dark.
I see each inlet inked in sweet, black line.
I draw the world that other eyes reveal:
the foreign shores I've never stood upon.
Perhaps I only see you now you're gone
and draw you only to believe you're real,
to feel your body close and think it mine.

The night's horizon line conceals your form
but only amplifies the breakers' roar.
The night is heavy on my chest and warm
and rocks me slowly closer to that shore.

Tranq's for the memory

She wanted to believe that something lasted
beyond its cycle—love, cut flowers, spring—
and waited for the telephone to ring:
got dressed got taken out got pretty plastered
got fucked got sad got scared got home alone.
She took a brand of sleep and fell into
a lidless spiral, watching fogged outtakes
of here and then—new dreams of old mistakes—
until the blackness split her head in two
and in she tumbled, grateful as a stone.

The days begin to shorten, nights to cool.
The summer turns to booze and drugs to cope.
The stars shine sullenly and work to rule.
She doesn't look to windows for her hope.

Sunday Morning

(First time for everything)

Unorthodox, this love. No prayers, no bells,
the only candles burning in my belly,
and every act of worship is an act
of tact, dissembling, watching, playing actor,
and in my heart, the music no one hears,
with words to my forgotten, hidden hymn,
small clouds in sense, as soft as pain and whimsy,
as you, a statue in that distant niche
of memory, of hunger's aching need,
of love that comes in wingbeats, love that nears.

I will not stand to sing this morning's song;
I'll whisper it. I'll hear it in my head,
and if, by chance, God hears, he'll get it wrong—
first time for everything, as he once said.

Sleek

The quality of water: sleek. Your skin
is poured around your body, smooth as oil,
the flow of air around an aerofoil,
a seal in water, notes as you begin
a gentle scat with bass and clarinet,
a cat before the fireplace: you're sleek,
a silky dress that licks around your hips,
the caramel of glance, the syruped lips
that sculpt your breath to shape the words you speak;
you're smooth as flame, you're soft, you're warm, you're wet.

A muscled movement glimpsed through undergrowth;
a liquid curve, the sway, the swerves, the turns;
the something learnt by each that's known to both:
you're sleek: your body is like oil: it burns.

Orthodox Christmas Card

The magi bought straight from the registry
which meant the rest were left to hum and haw
and mumble, shuffling sandalled feet in straw,
to wish the god-child — what? — longevity?
Why's only half the story ever told?
The myrrh and frankincense went up in smoke
but how did Joe and Mary then dispose
of all the gold? The truth is, no one knows,
but humble baby Jesus? What a joke!
The kid was loaded, like the dice Dad rolled.

This Christmas card may come a little late—
it might just feed your green recycling bin—
but know I took the time to contemplate
the miracle of birth devoid of sin.

The secret island

Red Rocks, February 2013

Beyond the season—past the sub-let sites,
the fold out couches and the weekly rents,
the front yards full of family friends in tents,
the music in the plover-startled nights—
the secret island dreams itself awake.
The waking is a tidal change of mood,
the reassertion of a silent will:
the heartbeat slows, the lungs expand and fill;
and everywhere discloses solitude,
the singleness it takes all things to make.

Tonight the sunset lights an orange sky
between two smokey charcoal limbs of land.
The gulls are black as crows as home they fly,
and I lie, losing warmth to night and sand.

Poem for my children

I wrote a poem for you all and lost it.
I can't remember now a single line,
which means it must have been the best of mine
since that one which I gave to ___ and she tossed it
in a drawer, or pocket, bin, left on a tram...
I sort of wish it mattered. Sort of don't.
My poems rise like swamp gas, flake like rust,
like tired footsteps agitating dust,
like conjured metaphors that won't.
I like to think I'm brilliant when I am.

If I could leave you anything, you know
I wouldn't leave you. But I do and will.
No words change that, but loss at least lasts till
we don't arrive at where we're going to go.

Instructions for loneliness

A self-help guide for the gregarious and socially adept

You can be lonely. Even you. Someone
like you. You may have thought you had to be
a poet, artist, thinker... but you don't.
The stupid and the popular, the least
profound can all aspire to loneliness:
this poem shows you how. I don't say it
is easy—not for all. I don't say you
won't still have moments when find you've touched
another's soul. We all have days like that.
But lonely's still a realistic goal.

Step One. Remove yourself and shut your eyes
and think of how you failed and why. Now breathe...
and think of who you're hurting with your life.
Now, think of no way out. And that's Step Two.

Worm

(Death Notice)

The worm is that worst secret: known well, but
which everybody thinks their own alone
and feels the secret gnawing into bone,
adrift in flesh and anchoring in gut.
The worm digests us, hour by painful hour.
The worm jaws move in peristaltic waves,
methodical tick tocks, relentless, insate.
Deliver us our pain and call it fate,
and help us spend the lives that no one saves,
for thine, worm, is the kingdom, thine the power.

There's nothing different about today.
Through all lives runs a single, sooty thread:
you lose your glasses, spill your coffee, say
the inappropriate about the dead.

In this box

The opportunities for talk are few.
Well, none. Thought has to be enough. That's good.
And touch, of course, is limited to wood,
which means I never think I'm touching you.
The dark itself is easy to accept.
The sounds are strange at first. You hear the tick
of time itself in murmurings of earth,
the lick of tiny tongues, cells giving birth
to cell selves, feet and cilia, the click
of tiny jaws. You wait. Then you expect.

The time will come, but never fast enough,
but never with the flash of light, the blare
of horns, the thick confetti rain of stuff.
The time will come with running out of air.

Old car

(The organ donation sonnet)

One day, the old car simply never starts.
The engine turns, perhaps, but doesn't fire.
Exhaustless, it's elected to retire
from being car to being spare car parts.
I, too, have signed the organ donor card.
I wait for my election to the host
when body parts of mine that won't be missed
are sewn into whoever's on the list.
I only hope who gets them needs them most
because no parts of mine were worked too hard.

I'd like to leave you something, too. What's there
that might help you to carry on when I'm
harp-strumming/roasting, long past earthly care?
The time we spent and wasted. Keep that time.

Quantum State

    Advice and sympathy are equally
repellent. Keep those soothing noises stuck
fast in your gullet. Hope for better luck
yourself and doze off through my shabby story,
but don't hang up. I need telecommunion.
    Until you've been a paunchy, middle-aged
disingénue in love you've never been
a fool, because fool is a quantum state between
which and all others decades of mismanaged
entropy and worship of illusion.

I stand exposed. I know it isn't pretty:
flesh hanging in unmuscled mass on bone;
a clotted mind, thrombosed with guilt, self-pity,
and pique; ears buzzing with the busy tone.

Well, fuck the fans of Keats

The fans of Keats read Shelley once, to weep
for their lost boy, the Peter Pan who tripped
before the ticking crocodile and dipped
out badly. Here's a secret I won't keep:
They skim. They do. Confront them and they blush.
The fans of Keats read Shelley once, to say
they've read it and to pass exams or find
a line that no one else is using, mind
you, one used in a last year's class is okay;
let nothing keep them too long from their crush.

I walked out in the early morning sun;
its warmth eased through me, sudden, single malt.
To readers, hello from another one,
    to fans of Keats, shouldn't you be doing something more important? Like your hair?

You

You cause the day. Your cloudy mornings kiss
my eyes, your soft grey light upon my lips;
the bed clothes stroke my skin like fingertips;
your body warmth is mine, and yours is this:
the sunlight seeping past an edge of curtain.
You populate my garden, morning Eve,
with many-jointed-legged things that spin
and crawl and fly and spawn like thoughts within
a dozy head, like kisses that you leave
on sleeping lips, like something vague and certain.

Your breath is breathing through my lungs;
I feel your gentle rhythm in my heart
and hear your song sung on a thousand tongues
and join the song. You cause my day to start.

Renaissance Music

I play the maudlin. It's a quaint old thing,
a bit lute-like with fewer strings, a lot
of frets ('fretfully hard'). It's also got
a strange sound board which makes a whining ring
so every note is like a whimpered cry.
I take my place beside the snivel and
the bass grimace, in front of our tantrum
(a strange, sporadic beat, unlike a drum)
and that completes my early music band.
I've got our new CD here. Care to buy?

I like to listen to it as I drive
to work; it soothes away the traffic pain.
I'm never more excited, more alive,
than when I hear that maudlin's sweet refrain.

The Barnacle

Just one death—not a nation or a race—
a drunk who kept his trousers up with string,
a barnacle upon the ship of state,
a name, a history, not worth preserving.
   He stank of old sweat, piss, and cheap sweet sherry.
The portal vein had swollen like a hawser
until today. The varices went pop
and pints of blood surprised this morning's corpse;
blood ran like rats before an open seacock:
   and off he bobbed to foul another ferry.

Somebody found him. Someone came and hosed
away the bloodstains of his final act.
His ashes will be buried. It's supposed
he had no kin. Someone records the fact.

Woman exercising on Red Rocks beach

Who answers your erratic semaphore?
Who's watching? Who interprets each wide loop
and wave, the wild extensions as you stoop
and stretch. Who watches, and from which imagined shore?
    She reads her answer in a patterned sea,
in Jesus holes appearing in the clouds,
in flocks of terns that splinter silver sherds
from waves, in white caps, sea wrack, secret words
the beach confides to her alone aloud:
    the everything and all that isn't me.

Exact, astatic, jointed, this strange dance
might be a ritual another age
could understand. She is her circumstance:
a song bird singing its elaborate cage.

Butcher Birds

The butcher birds are singing bloody joy
for spring, for morning, other nesting birds
and fledglings, warm as other lovers' words,
as certain as a certain girl meets boy.
My bloodied heart is sliding down your throat.
I dangle, forked in your selected tree,
awaiting you, your hunger or your what
the hell, and feel you fall upon me, hot,
impatient, ready to be having me
and singing every morning's every note.

You're visiting, I know, each day afresh.
You haven't come for honey, bread, or bird bath.
You have my trust. I offer it in flesh.
I understand your purpose and your path.

I walk your legs

Sometimes I walk your legs to where I sit
and let myself admire them, touch them, feel
the velvet inner thighs, let fingers steal
into the secret warmth of cunt and clit,
and pull your body closer to my face.
Sometimes I touch your fingers to your hips
and push your singlet up, and let them feel
the curve of breasts and chest and then reveal
your nipples hungering for tongue and lips.
My longing lengthens over time and space.

The violence of longing is self-crime
achieving nothing but the worst self-waste,
a sack of being, leaking shit and time,
and longing for your touch and smell and taste.

Three Thirds of a Day Without You

1/3

They reach agreement in the stray grey lights
of morning once again; another night's
negotiations over, treaties signed,
and wary lovers wearily remind
themselves of other selves. Keys turn in locks.
This is the time road-sweepers whisk a thousand,
um, indiscretions into features: mouths and
unopened eyes; a thousand bodies fill
the cold moulds of their last night's clothes and chill;
and faces face back in a thousand clocks.

You should be here to leave now; this is when
most lovers choose to part: too cold for guilt,
too late for dates more certain than again;
when love is turned down like the bloody quilt...

2/3

Don't blame the sun if it's got better things
to do. Lay off the starlings, too. They sing,
all right, like starlings—certainly well meant—
and if there's grass, it's cracks in the cement...
Well, Christ! a city winter after all.
Forget the cars' exhaust, the fumes that drift
from flues and vents; the air will soon change shift:
let's let it. Why regret the lack of church bells,
snow-bells, bellbirds? They're somewhere. Somewhere else.
With you? Somewhere. The wrong side of recall.

The bees are fumbling into flowers there;
each garden has its own blackbird to sing
of lawns and fruit trees, picket fences, clean air;
so who's to blame if winter isn't spring...

3/3

The moon might be a street light, might stay low
and never move, tough luck for Galileo;
behind the clouds who knows if there are stars?
The gutters play the same old grating twelve bars,
and any passing cab might bring you soon.
A moth is dying in the iron lace;
small fingernails of rain mark time and place,
like wing-beats in the webs no brooms can reach,
like rain, those quiet words of foreign speech,
like rain-shot puddles shattering the moon.

Perhaps you're listening to your sisters somewhere,
the heady perfume of their common sense;
the street lights flower through wax-paper air
like moons, dissolving into radiance…

The Apology

for Kevin Rudd and all you other gormless fuckers

When does the sun get tired, looking down
on yet another brand new day for this
strange ape-race, gibbering the same old pish
and kicking all the same ideas around
and changing nothing? Nothing, yet again.
The emperor announces nakedness,
and naked, all applaud, as if our skin
was our excuse—forgive us everything
and let's pretend we like the fucking mess
we've made, because we'd do it all again.

Allow me just to say—and take this in
the spirit in which it's offered—fuck you all.
And take the mealy future you foresee
and shove it. Spare me and the sun the sight.

VA 894

Georgina, flight attendant on the plane
to Melbourne, who is far too beautiful
for any man in 30D to pull,
prepares her demonstration to explain
the safety features. I can only stare.
She stands, the goddess of the aircraft aisle,
an act of prayer made of this routine task:
life jacket, safety card, seat belt, and mask;
rewarding the attentive with her smile,
dismissing the dismissive to the air.

Gods keep their distance from us. She's the same,
now somewhere thirty thousand feet above me.
You don't chase Gods; you just worship the name:
Georgina, Goddess who will never love me.

The Opening of the New Parliament House by H.R.H. Queen Elizabeth II

1

The Queen looks down on Canberra and thinks
of Maya, Inca, Aztec—in a handful
of centuries this city will be a find
the most impressive ruin in the land.
    She puts her specs back on, looks through her speech.
What will they make of it? Will tourists send
back postcards having done the major sites,
found burly symbols in the ancient plan,
and puzzled at its star and circle streets?
    She wonders what this place will have to teach.

Australian accents still surprise the Queen;
the tender handshakes they're so quick to release.
They treat her like the Doulton figurine
upon a packing-case board mantelpiece.

2

The Queen unlocks the door and frames her face
in plate glass ready to express delight.
Her famous face. Her smile. Her famous wave.
She feels as common as a two bob bit
   and steps inside and only wants to laugh:
it's done up like a flash department store
in coloured marble, wood, and shiny brass!
They've bought. Bought everything they could afford,
like children with a parent's credit card.
   She finds her voice, "It's not been done by half!"

She understands the silly flagpole now—
its own apology, if rightly viewed.
The people of a squat land can't allow
their standards to have too much altitude.

3

The Queen unveils the Queen of years to come—
a pretty horrible herself in bronze;
the hard, shot-peppered visage of a woman
whose frown and wrinkled lip are not a sovereign's.
   Look on their works! They have so much to show:
a tapestry of native forest hacked
away to keep connecting doorways whole;
the two chambers; the gallery of chaps
whose consciences were also done in oils.
   All built to mob-scale for the overthrow.

She likes Australians. They make no demands.
They build their castles with a childish pride,
upending pails on lone and level sands,
as blankly purposeful as wind and tide.

Sometimes I'm tired

Sometimes I'm tired—body is a weight.
My brain is stepped; my thoughts are footfalls, footsteps.
My mind is clumsy as a pair of forceps:
I try to pick up buttons from a plate.
I try and fail and fail to understand.
To think is not to feel; to feel is not
to understand; to understand is not
to know; to know is not to have faith; not
to have faith is to not have what you've got.
Too tired to tell the lie I cannot stand.

I hear your sleepy voice and smell your scent.
Your body is a beacon, guiding mark
of infrared, of warmth, of where love went,
of how light only penetrates the dark.

A week's awakenings in seven couplets

Mon
>The morning is a shattered cup. I chance
>bare footfalls in a slow and watchful dance.

Tues
>The birdsong's absence registers before
>I wake. I wake to rain and nothing more.

Wed
>Awareness takes its first, slow sips of sight
>in fine bone china cups of milky light.

Thurs
>The city breathes its low, subsonic roar.
>Long waveforms break along a distant shore.

Fri
>Before alarm, my thoughts are sung by birds,
>and then my brain is battered into words.

Sat
>Moon sliver, grey-blue clouds, a lemon smear
>of watercolour sky. Welcome to here.

Sun
>A wave receding on the sand leaves shown
>the moment: fragment shells and weed and stone.

A Hopeless Land

(Sufficient Rope)

In that imagined land the children hope
until they're old enough to act and know
that Santa is an honest fraud. They grow
to work and earn themselves sufficient rope.
Ideals are framed and hung on every wall.
The heroes of that land are sharp enough
to gorge and wax as fat as other adders,
insinuate their way up corporate ladders,
and keep their consciences as clear as slough;
rogue musketeers whose cry is, Free-for-all!

At night the land is lost: a fog of dreams
arises from its swamps of thick intrigue.
We dream of change. Asleep, it almost seems
as possible as yesterday's fatigue.

Five white shirts

Tick off the days. Another working week
lies crumpled on the floor in five white shirts.
The start of something ending always hurts;
and this is no exception. My technique
is just to lie and smile and say I'm fine.
Each day another layer peels away.
Another, softer layer lies exposed
and nothing is revealed; it's just unclothed.
You don't call. I have nothing left to say.
Tomorrow finds me hanging on the line.

Recuperation days are largely still.
I keep myself from sleep and lie awake.
New days line up, white dashes up a hill.
I count them off with every step I take.

Don't Worry, Bob

Ambition always was a garbage truck.
It calls at intervals along your street
and levies each house for its share of muck;
forever full, forever unreplete.
    Corruption always had a complex perfume.
For every action there is equal waste,
a sewage: effort, time, and breath. Ambition's
favourite morsel leaves the sourest taste;
consuming men, excreting politicians:
    a thin manure that starves the smallest bloom.

Some dot the paddocks, some float out to sea,
die on the job, or represent the Queen,
some land on boulevards of gay Paris—
the same by-products that they've always been.

Today

(like every other)

It's just
as well we haven't met
today I wouldn't know what to say you'd say
you're looking well while I was looking
for a café and you'd say I can't stop anyway
smile
and pass the briefest time of day
and goodbye good to meet and I would walk
the other way or cross the street.

Dragged ragged over bitumen
beneath a thousand stranger soles than mine
my shadow's wearing thin avoiding you
too successfully to be trying to.
Pause: amazing all the faces that aren't yours.

Body over time

Ridiculously beautiful you stretch
your body long along the bed and turn
and ask me, "What do you expect to learn?"
I wring my brain for reasons it can fetch,
excuses to explain this fascination.
My study is your body over time:
its swellings and its falls, the tiny marks,
the lines like tidal lines, the pales and darks.
Perfection doesn't have a paradigm:
it fuels all living, all imagination.

You think your beauty brief, time unforgiving.
You're wrong. There is no particle of song,
no moment you can say is love. All living,
all beauty is a process. And it's long.

Noosa Beach Retiree

Once more the age old foes face off together:
sun-hatted toddler; wary silver gull.
The ancient, human ache to steal a feather,
to touch, to hold, to own, years never dull,
but toddler falls, or gull takes flight in fear.
I, like the rest, have come up here to live
the few remaining years of pointlessness
in pilfered comfort, trusting these years give
excuse, apply a lacquer of success
to those before. Up here, it's all veneer.

We recognise and label patterns: tide
and currents, seasons, moon and stars; we trace
their motions, actions, orbits, but we hide
the emptiness in which it all takes place.

Only Scum

self-portrait on a blank canvas

I always thought to rescue something from
the crowded isolation of existing,
thought something might ignite by my persisting;
a fizzer bigger than a sherbet bomb,
and nothing comes from nothing, that's assured.
You ask me to reveal myself, but how?
It's nothing I conceal. There's nothing there.
I'm just a mass in space, displacing air,
that's seriously empty, stern to prow.
I'm one of nature's vacuums: all abhorred...

More dreary self-reviling, roll your eyes,
ignore it and go back the way you've come.
You got this far; it can't be a surprise
to find that froth and bubble 's only scum.

Painter, retrospective

(Nothing has its place)

My life is governed by two axes: Ex
and Why. I plot the exes to explore
the whys, revealing graphically there's more
to choice than temperament and chance and sex:
the fundamental need to make a mess.
Set up the pins to knock them down. Deface
the walls. Turn up the amp; distort the sound.
First build, then raze the temple to the ground.
The de/con struction: nothing has its place
and joy dissolves in puddles of distress.

My watercolours mix and turn to brown,
some dark, some light, but all a shade of murk.
Unmeaning viewed from left, right, upside down,
these dirty smears. That's all. A whole life's work.

Aphantasia in Geneva

It would be worth remembering this scene:
the mountains in the background, lit with cloud,
the lake, sail-speckled, beach paved with the towels
of families and lovers. What would it mean
to conjure this scene any day or night?
For hundreds here, who sit like me and stare,
this is a pictured memory. For me,
it's gone. Gone with its moment. What I see
dissolves to words not worth the time to share.
I envy you that magic double sight.

For me there is no magic lantern show:
the past is an uncoloured, dot point list.
So please assure me, every time you go,
the future past you plan should not to be missed.

Your presence

Your presents wink at me through gift shop glass,
in jewellers' windows, in department store
displays: I check the price. It's always more
than I can bet or throw away. I pass.
And yet I wrap them for you in my mind.
You walk beside me as I'm walking through
the streets, and laugh when I ask what you'd wear.
You tell me, Better ask me when I'm there.
Your absence is as hard to please as you,
but all these things are yours, all that I find.

If ever you leave me, I won't know what
to do in London, Paris, Prague. I'll stop,
'coz you're the one attraction they've all got:
I could be here with you. Come on. Let's shop.

The Doctor's Garden

The doctor has a garden full of healing
(imagine for yourself the way it looks)
where she consults her patients, not the books,
and they, so self-assuredly unfeeling,
prescribe their cure—coincidentally hers.
The chives bloom mauve, the parsley runs to seed,
the thyme trespasses on the path; she says
she doesn't hold with single purposes,
and digs out native violets like weeds,
transfers them to a bed that she prefers.

She plants herself beside the apricot,
admires its teardrop leaves through half-closed eyes,
recalls a few odd jobs that she forgot,
and gardener and garden synthesise.

Index of first lines

A helicopter chops a potentate ... 61
Accept for fourteen lines the proposition: ... 220
Adored wife and the armour that I wear, ... 77
Advice and sympathy are equally ... 233
All right, you bastard bloody thing, you've beaten me. ... 42
All right. I wasn't always faithful; nor ... 60
Already last week's paper—so remote ... 85
Ambition always was a garbage truck. ... 253
And as you age and gather adjectives ... 216
And Mars replies without words. Mars replies ... 106
And on a later day, God looked again ... 10
Another day of our farewell. A process ... 205
Around and round we go and never find ... 91
Around the neon-lit advertisements ... 214
As I lay dying, I remembered you. ... 46
As I'm incapable of love, instead, ... 201
As worker states collapse, the socialist ... 144
Australians all, we may as well rejoice ... 108
Because I woke up early, I went walking, ... 211
Behind the mirror, small, among the shoes, ... 161
Believe I think of you believing I ... 83
Beyond the season—past the sub-let sites, ... 227
But don't you wish that God himself had thought ... 136
But this is not the time to think; this is ... 111
Careers are over-rated. Set your sights ... 118
Comrades! The call to strike is a mistake! ... 78
Could anyone be bothered pressing these ... 164
Couldn't be easier. As easy as ... 20
Cross little faces singing their complaint: ... 43
Dear Clive, I'm sorry you can't visit; so, ... 13
Dear God, let me be missing, crumbled dust, ... 12
Dear God, please let there be at least a type ... 193
Dear Granddad Mullens, whom I never knew, ... 66
Deception is the cloth, the cloak I wear, ... 207
Don't have to drink to stumble down this street; ... 188
Don't let me die. Not here. Not where I've spent ... 176
Don't make the desert's worst mistake, mistake ... 69
Don't think, because I never wear a cape, ... 50
Each generation has to learn to say ... 132
Each week another youless month goes past. ... 147
Eleven minutes later things had changed. ... 100
Eternal love is brief and hurts forever. ... 102
Experience has taught you how to look ... 24
For every nail their hammers tapped into ... 122
For thy sweet love remembered is a knife, ... 90
Georgina, flight attendant on the plane ... 245
Give us again our daily piece of toast; ... 133
Had I returned and told the things I saw, ... 110

He lies there, curled up like a moon; the moon—	129
He photographs. I write. The same absurd	120
Heart sick, brain sick, soul sick. I cannot live	63
Her body sprinkles adjectives behind	191
Her clothes are one of her obsessions. I'm	51
Her conifers are military trees.	198
Here is where the homeless heart is stuck	68
Hey star girl! Where you heading now? And where	62
I always thought to rescue something from	257
I don't know if it saved me or just failed	103
I don't remember faces well, it's true.	47
I flew to Hampstead Heath so I could lie	148
I know I'm heading where you've gone. I feel	104
I lived for art and died art-broken, Callas,	194
I miss the ideal that I made of you.	189
I need a sign: THIS ISN'T LOVE, okay?	58
I occupy the park bench long enough	177
I play the maudlin. It's a quaint old thing,	236
I saw the best lines of my generation	26
I see you and the scales form on my eyes:	23
I shaped my flints. I lived in caves as well.	138
I spare a thought tonight for all the rich	131
I spit on Charity. I spit on fools	117
I want to set the final full stop—pop!—	185
I wear a sympathy with night: I'm black.	123
I wrote a poem for you all and lost it.	228
I'm chasing you, if only slowly; I'm	28
I'm fading: faster than my hair grows grey;	3
I'm not unfaithful to my wife; the girl	11
I'm parked. I close my eyes. I wait. It's coming.	180
I'm staying here—immovable as debt.	17
I'm washed up, dead, sea-spat upon this shore,	48
I'm bungee walking round the streets. That line	141
Impossibly innocuous, it comes	45
In Berlin they can stomach them. So where's	64
In case it rains for twenty years or more,	101
In his hands I was beautiful. He made	135
In that imagined land the children hope	251
Incinerate me. Turn it on me. Let	184
Is this condition possible? I thought	134
Is this what separates us? Have I found	186
It isn't easy—neither of us being real:	149
It isn't Paris and it isn't Prague.	179
It knows the words it thinks I should have sent.	202
It might be sanskrit, or a whisper heard	215
It must be spring. The pubs are turning into	86
It orbits and it shines a silver light	70
It started just like every other day:	130
It tastes like foetal blood miscarried	84
It would be worth remembering this scene:	259
It's been a long time since I felt like this,	75
It's Christmas Eve and everything is shut	182
It's just	254

It's just a game: we hide; we seek; we find; ... 34
It's just another blackbird in the leaves ... 41
It's rubble now. The thousands of our hours, ... 204
It's there again. The world. It's back. The leaves ... 22
It's very like the periodic table: ... 79
It's complicated. Someone has to talk. ... 1
I've spent my life. Not well or wisely. Not ... 76
Josh wears the woad of serial defeat ... 94
Just ice without the alcohol, just speed ... 27
Just one death—not a nation or a race— ... 237
Just walk with me where rock shelves poke red tongues ... 55
Kristine, because I lost the poems and ... 166
Leave me the knife you use to pare your fruit, ... 139
Les says that he was fat, and I believe ... 113
Let's spoon. Let's fork. Let's never, ever knife. ... 172
Lie down, roll over, show your private parts, ... 156
Lost and confounded; behind the ifs and buts, ... 175
Love sings of love undying even as ... 7
Love, it's a lost art. No one knows the craft. ... 8
Melancholy: stations do a good ... 33
My children send me postcards from a land ... 25
My dear, ambiguous God/poet/ess, ... 21
My face is like old undies: the elastic ... 81
My life is governed by two axes: Ex ... 258
Not being seventeen means suicide ... 98
Not much worth ending ever finished at ... 197
Of course, the train starts pulling out while we're ... 4
Once more the age old foes face off together: ... 256
One day the news will break from Hollywood: ... 116
One day, the old car simply never starts. ... 232
Pack everything you want to leave behind ... 36
Paralysis is still the teddy bear ... 196
Preserved as I was broken: wings awry; ... 96
Preserved in lines of sedimentary verse ... 88
Receive this tiny burden and believe ... 107
Regrets? I've had a feud with my past life. ... 53
Returning virgins, each sunrise renews ... 151
Ridiculously beautiful you stretch ... 255
Rouse the lazy buggers from their bed! ... 140
Sex took sabbatical when it was due; ... 167
She doesn't bother with the artful use ... 169
She lets me touch her honey skin. She calls ... 87
She says, The time comes when we all escape ... 170
She tips her head back when we kiss: it's Pez. ... 171
She wanted to believe that something lasted ... 223
She was an angel once—she didn't seem: ... 152
She'll never have to see bits missing from ... 209
So go. But understand you'll never know ... 39
So now the rain decides to tumble down, ... 40
so somewhere in the world it's half past twelve, ... 29
So sugar muse me, make me take it on ... 199
Some things are absolute and some are true. ... 150
Sometimes I walk your legs to where I sit ... 240

Sometimes I'm tired—body is a weight.	249
Teach me to dance, sharp as a silhouette,	109
That's it. The place that launched a thousand miserable careers. I hadn't thought	6
The biggest moon in eighteen years dissolves	157
The butcher birds are singing bloody joy	239
The crickets trill like geiger counters, stopping	15
The day assumes an eeriness, the light	203
The day that daylight saving ends and I'm	18
The doctor has a garden full of healing	261
The dry stone wall is built of many rocks,	38
The dull ache of the missing part you know	143
The everlasting universe of things,	19
The falconer removes the hood: a simple move	210
The fans of Keats read Shelley once, to weep	234
The getting lost is easy, even after	195
The how is easy to explain, but dull;	146
The line your skin makes breaking water marks	222
The magi bought straight from the registry	226
The mail lands in the middle of the hall	125
The moon, as dogged as an albatross,	153
The morning is a shattered cup. I chance	250
The mothers ask their simple question: why	187
The only life I've left is locked in your	67
The only star—of course, it's not a star—	9
The opportunities for talk are few.	231
The other men will catch the spiders in	183
The parents watch the tele while the kids	71
The perfect black dress is—does nothing more	213
The psych test shows I'm one of those they call	127
The quality of water: sleek. Your skin	225
The Queen looks down on Canberra and thinks	246
The rest are wasting time: your own (don't care)	93
The river Derci flows across our maps,	154
The same herbs that cured nothing then are still	217
The Sheffield soot is being washed away.	74
The sky is filled unhurriedly with cloud,	174
The statuary was only ever made	192
The street is full; unnoticed miracles	49
The third day that the keepers haven't been.	137
The universe is full of wheels. Count five	114
The unseen lines draw you, and you are made,	73
The weather is a Rubik's cube. Rain falls	112
The woman tracing her erratic way	30
The worm is that worst secret: known well, but	230
The X waits like a spider in the dark	52
There is a state beyond pain when the mind	126
There's nothing for the kitchen or the car	219
These are not words. These are the shadows cast	57
They catch no fish and watch a grim bay dish	165
They reach agreement in the stray grey lights	241
They sting: the lines you sing when things are dark;	65
This dance—this tapping on the keys, these hands	44
This is a very human trait: we sort,	16

This is my work, and if it seems to you	119
This is the first of fourteen lines that won't	2
This is your poem, written in a tongue	14
This journey starts without a leaving and	37
This might work: tear them, like you tear a sheet	56
This poem's ordinary. This is yours.	163
Tick off the days. Another working week	252
To people of Australia I bequeath	124
Ulysses dogs us down the night soil lane,	221
Unorthodox, this love. No prayers, no bells,	224
We both know you're not reading this and I'm	31
We carry hesitation wounds around,	142
We drown in Golden Syrup, amber goo;	206
We shelter in our bodies while the storm	121
Well, one of us is widely read, of course.	173
What fragment of a universal plan	168
What's that? What's hiding in your kitchen clutter?	54
Whatever had to have been cannot be.	89
When does the sun get tired, looking down	244
When I was younger and could fly by just	212
When other people die, I try to hide	218
When words run out, we look at pictures or	95
When you defined the rain as 'that which falls'	158
Where am I left? I must sometimes appear:	160
Where are you now? Where do I send this last	97
Who answers your erratic semaphore?	238
Who is it isn't moving there? Outside	155
Without a reader's card this library	80
Without your silver iteration birds	82
You can be lonely. Even you. Someone	229
You can't be serious. I haven't got	208
You cause the day. Your cloudy mornings kiss	235
You check, and everything is there, which means	159
You get depressed because you're stunning? What?	59
You have the letters, several alphabets	190
You may be ugly here: let out your belt.	128
You never lived this tidily. Not here;	5
You only know you've got it when your brain	92
You only use those legs to walk, but I	200
You rescued me with that kiss, syrup sweet,	162
You'd almost call me lonely if it wasn't	115
You'd think that no one ever went to Ghent.	145
You're never more than Google million miles	35
You're not alone when you are still alone.	72
You've got to love Australian girls abroad.	32
Your absence has the sting of single malt	105
Your Auntie Pauline has a Lego set,	178
Your footsteps scuffle down along the branches	99
Your legs eleven	181
Your presents wink at me through gift shop glass,	260

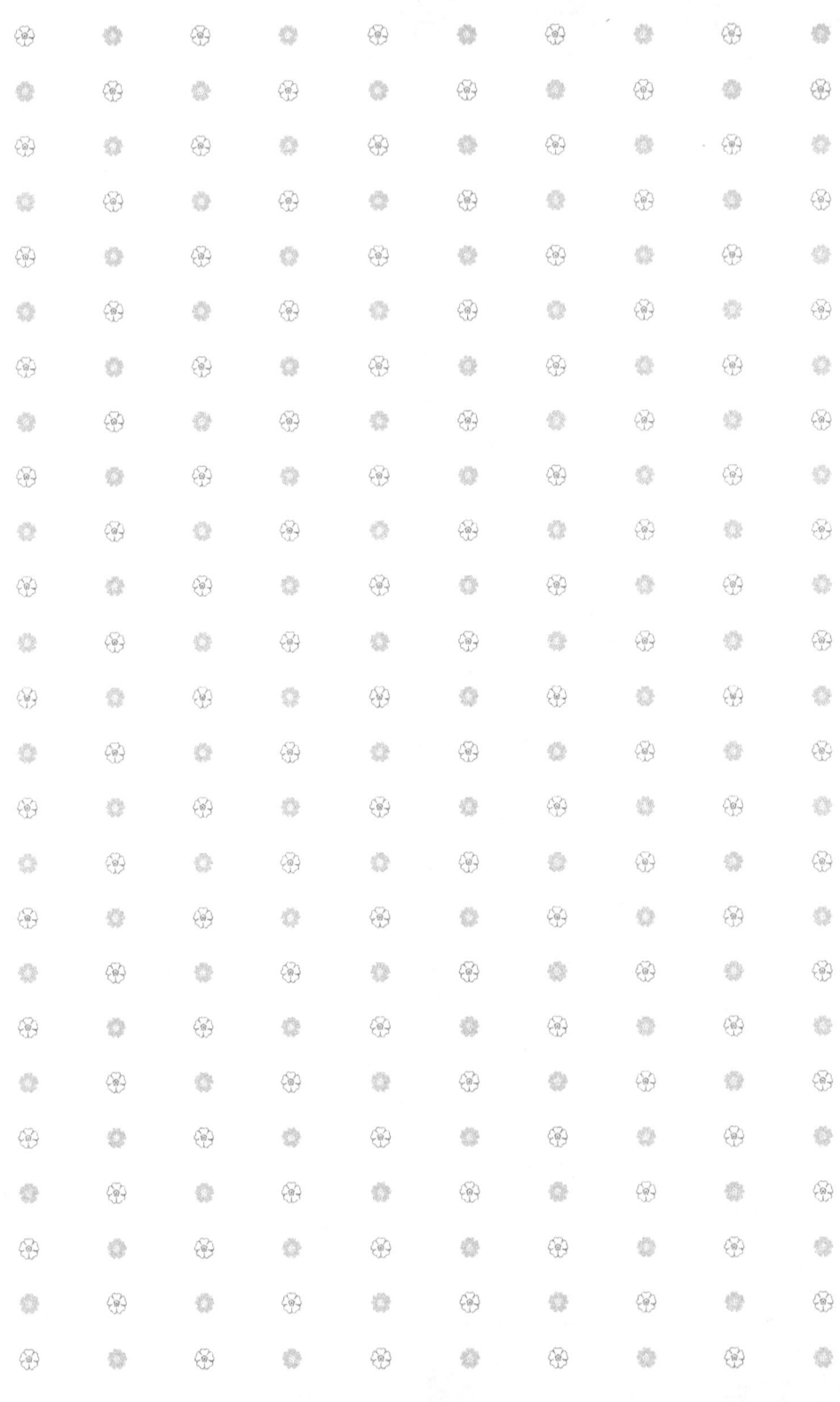